—— A Primer for Teaching Pacific Histories ——

DESIGN PRINCIPLES
FOR TEACHING HISTORY
A series edited by Antoinette Burton

A PRIMER FOR TEACHING PACIFIC HISTORIES

—— Ten Design Principles ——

Matt K. Matsuda

DUKE UNIVERSITY PRESS
Durham and London
2020

© 2020 Duke University Press
All rights reserved

Typeset in Garamond Premier Pro by
Tseng Information Systems, Inc.

Library of Congress Cataloging-in-Publication Data
Names: Matsuda, Matt K., author.
Title: A primer for teaching Pacific histories :
ten design principles / Matt K. Matsuda.
Description: Durham : Duke University Press, 2020. |
Series: Design principles for teaching history | Includes
bibliographical references and index.
Identifiers: LCCN 2019035460 (print)
LCCN 2019035461 (ebook)
ISBN 9781478007951 (hardcover)
ISBN 9781478008477 (paperback)
ISBN 9781478012115 (ebook)
Subjects: LCSH: Pacific Area—Study and teaching (Higher) |
Islands of the Pacific—Study and teaching (Higher)
Classification: LCC DU28.3 .M345 2020 (print) | LCC DU28.3
(ebook) | DDC 995.0071/1—dc23
LC record available at https://lccn.loc.gov/2019035460
LC ebook record available at https://lccn.loc.gov/2019035461

Cover art: John Pule, *Taumalala*, 2016. Oils, enamels,
inks, and polyurethane on canvas, 1520 × 1520 mm.
Image courtesy of Gow Langsford Gallery and John Pule.

Contents

Acknowledgments vii

Introduction: Objectives 1

PART I
LAYING FOUNDATIONS

One
Begin with the State of Our Knowledge 19

Two
Secure the Fundamentals:
Navigation, Diaspora, Settlement 25

Three
Underscore the Connections:
Encounters in the Contact Zone 33

Four
Review Disputed Legacies and Arguments 51

PART II
DEVISING STRATEGIES

Five
Imperialism as a Teaching Tool 67

Six
Anthropology and Ethnology as Teaching Tools 89

Seven
Conflict as a Teaching Tool 95

Eight
Identity as a Teaching Tool 105

───── PART III ─────
PERFORMED HISTORIES

Nine
Distinguish Representations and Realities 113

Ten
See the Process of Enacting Knowledge 121

Notes 145

Selected Bibliography 155

Index 161

—— *Acknowledgments* ——

A TEACHING VOLUME IS built around the work of other teachers—and all of our students. I recognize some of those who have taught me: Greg Dening, John Gillis, Epeli Hauʻofa, Teresia Teaiwa, Paul D'Arcy, Vilsoni Hereniko, Damon Salesa, and so many others past and present. I've understood that a work like this is not possible without opportunities to share ideas with colleagues and students around the world. I am indebted for the support—and invitations—from Georgine Clarsen, Ian Conrich, Geoff White, Martin Dusinberre, Patrick Manning, Robin Walz, Edward Slack, Marcus Rediker, Sarah Beringer, Thomas Schwarz, David Armitage, Alison Bashford, Beth Lew-Williams, Warwick Anderson, Evelyn Hu-Dehart, David Igler, Carlos Mondragon, and Dena Seidel. For their ideas and inspirations, I thank my colleagues, including Bronwen Douglas, Rainer Buschman, Anne Hattori, Judy Bennet, Ryan Jones, David Hanlon, J. Kehaulani Kauanui, Marjan Schwegman, Jaap Talsma, Takashi Fujitani, Kathleen Lopez, and Allan Punzalan Isaac. This volume has been made possible by the energy and vision of Antoinette Burton and Miriam Angress, for Duke University Press. It is for my family, for a great teacher—Michiko Matsuda—and for Lee Quinby, as always. And for my students, who have taught me what I and they need to know.

Introduction

OBJECTIVES

Begin with What You Think You Know

When I first entertained the notion of teaching something like Pacific histories, I had a different scholarly background, coming as I did out of more general global-comparative and European studies. With parents both born in the Hawaiian Islands to nineteenth-century immigrant Japanese, I thought I was familiar enough with Asia and the Pacific through personal family lore. This made me interested in other parts of the world — such as Europe, which was utterly unknown and outside my experience. And so I spent most of my early teaching and writing career in European studies — a fascinating realm — where I focused on historical memory, political cultures, and the constitution of global imperialism. The latter, especially, led me to reengage with the Pacific. By that time, I had spent decades pointedly studying other things and had learned to appreciate how little I knew about different histories, certainly Pacific histories. I asked myself: What is it I think I know, even before I begin? I soon discovered that much of my knowledge of this thing called "the Pacific" came from images, assumptions, stereotypes, and general narratives picked up from popular culture.

You, or your students, might very likely find yourselves in similar situations. Who is presumed to be the student—or teacher—is, naturally, an important launching question. The approach in what follows obeys a couple of assumptions. One is that the reader here is an instructor who might be considering the possibilities for teaching Pacific histories to a largely high school or undergraduate college audience, one with relatively little knowledge of Pacific histories as a subject or field. A volume like this one is intended less to provide comprehensive content than to offer my thinking about what scholars in a particular discipline consider to be useful examples or important questions. In my own case, in transitioning my teaching between overlapping but distinctive academic specialties, what I first most needed to know was what key issues framed major debates, questions, and shared understandings in Pacific and Oceanian studies.

Listening to my own colleagues, for example, I knew that scholars of the United States might, hypothetically, be initially at a loss if asked to teach the histories of the African continent, or Latin America. Asian specialists could, presumably, be uncomfortable if requested to describe Europe or the Middle East. And yet, you may be called upon to do just that, particularly in teaching programs dedicated to global or world perspectives. Of course, institutional duty isn't the only motivation to study the history of a particular area. All teachers have strong intellectual curiosities and over time may decide they want to expand their knowledge. For history teachers in particular, this generally means expanding one's subject matter by moving in time (say, from modern to medieval or ancient, or the reverse, toward the contemporary period) and in space, incorporating a potentially daunting array of cultures, civilizations, empires, and lines of transmission and influence drawn from around the globe. For many instructors, the Pacific has long been peripheral and only recently engaged—beyond obligatory gestures to East Asia—as a realm of teaching.

In my first efforts at teaching Pacific histories, I was well aware that the field was populated by great scholars and teachers from a stunning array of cultures who were born and resided in the places they studied, and had built scholarship out of not only research and erudition, but everyday engagements with communities, languages, and their own families, ancestors, and lived experiences. Those who wrote academic histories could have generated knowledge not just through research subjects, but by telling stories around questions formulated with neighbors and personal connections. You might wonder, as did I, how exactly one approaches a subject other than as an interloper. One answer is to acknowledge the outsider's perspective — with questions and openness. So, I thought, what might be some introductory frameworks for addressing the Pacific? It is necessary to become a student oneself, a learner, and step away for a moment from being the teacher. If we begin by assembling our Pacific histories, what are the fragments? They can be anything from popular culture to archival knowledge, cultural experience to scholarly analysis. This teaching approach can be particularly resonant when focalized through images, for these parts of the world often are not familiar enough for audiences to have visual references. I regularly let students exercise their understanding and imagination through received knowledge, stereotypes, or whatever they can think of: all become points of discussion. The point of teaching then becomes to shape, counterpoint, and correct where appropriate, and deepen these understandings.

Examples of such starting points that I often hear include islands with palm trees, neon and glass skyscrapers, harbors, tattoos and bodies, burning battleships at Pearl Harbor, undersea volcanoes, Polynesian voyaging canoes, mushroom clouds over Pacific atolls, container ships and passenger liners, littoral encounters between Islanders and outlanders, Japanese anime characters, banquets of Chinese cuisine, submerged islands, monolithic architecture and stone ruins, ancient temples, sugarcane plantations, San Francisco gold miners, Spanish galleons . . . the list is inexhaustible. Are any of these "wrong"? No, certainly. The point, though, is to rescue them from the merely anecdotal or the simple image or stereotype and reincorporate them into a wider comparative and analytic understanding.

The idea here is not to present a catalog or even an overview, but to immediately frame the state of our knowledge. Regarding the Pacific, what narratives and tropes are already familiar and accessible?[1] Many students will claim they don't know any, but in fact they do: the Pacific War, islands and paradise, cannibals and missionaries, the Pacific Rim and Asian tigers, consumer goods and touristic representations. Teaching this way organizes inquiries around the principle of what we think we know—beginning not with the historical record and evidence, but with received wisdom and imaginings. Through this, questions can develop, such as, what do we conjure or pull from deep cultural references about the Pacific? Be aware and even reassured that neither scholars nor even inhabitants of the region necessarily agree about the defining parameters. More specifically, how has the Pacific been differently imagined from west to east, and east to west (or north to south)?

The Pacific can be understood as denominated through a number of big stories, even while no standard approach has yet evolved. From a time of ancient migrations and seaborne empires to one of trade and global power with the Chinese (Zheng He's Treasure Fleets), then the Portuguese, Dutch, and Spanish (following Vasco da Gama, Cornelis de Houtmann, and Ferdinand Magellan), the bigger picture has constantly shifted. By the eighteenth century, the site of the search for souls and treasure was reimagined as an eighteenth-century paradise for Enlightenment Europe and then despoiled by the encroachments of traders, missionaries, and military forces—though the idyllic imaginary remains the constant in modern tourism. By the middle of the nineteenth century, an age of European empire was in full force, with conquests from Tahiti to Canton and settler colonies stretching across Australia, New Zealand, Fiji, Hawai'i, the Philippines, and California.

The late nineteenth and early twentieth centuries marked the Pacific as a theater of global warfare, beginning in East Asia, from the Sino-Japanese and Russo-Japanese conflicts, spreading through Korea, Taiwan, and coastal China and the Philippines to Singapore, New Guinea, the Solomon Islands, Guam, and the Marshall Islands. The United States recognizes the primacy of Pearl Harbor in the struggle, as well as Iwo Jima, just as the Japanese underscore the atomic bombings of Hiroshima and Nagasaki.

The later twentieth and twenty-first centuries are marked by postwar colonial legacies and sovereignty struggles, from China and Vietnam to New Caledonia and the Solomon Islands, claims for redress from indigenous peoples, and issues of global impact: nuclear testing and environmental destruction, including overfishing, coral bleaching, and rising waters due to climate change. Concomitantly, this has also been the moment of the postwar eminence of the Japanese export economy, superseded by China as a political and foreign investment behemoth, and the spread of Asian consumer products and popular culture all around the world. Questions remain as to whether the globe faces a Pacific Century. All of these issues address the main points about how I might underscore key elements, themes, events, and stories in an introductory approach. My point here, however, is not to determine a standard narrative but to indicate precisely that the Pacific is a subject that must be defined, assembled, shaped, and bounded before it can be discussed.

You might notice that in the above paragraphs I have organized my touchstones around the most venerable of historical conventions: chronology. Ancient migrations and treasure fleets are located in a time recorded in archaeological and early documentary records, moving up through an early modern, Enlightenment, colonial, and then Pacific Century narrative. Still, the work need not be followed or employed in a linear fashion. Teachers interested in general knowledge from archaeology, folklore, linguistics, and the ancient Pacific can focus first on the early sections. Instructors more concerned about postcolonial and contemporary sovereignty and identity struggles can begin later in the narrative.

Perhaps the most interesting teaching experiences come, to my view, where these intersect, for example, in discussing the ways that twentieth-century anthropological studies of Pacific peoples still framed cultures as somehow primitive or surviving from primordial ages, or the ways that archaeological sites and ancestral remains become points of debate and political contest between indigenous communities, museums, and scientific researchers. Any section or chapter can be unpacked by theme, evidence, or example. As a teacher, I favor consistently relating the past and present to each other, and in what follows I have presented an array of particular cases that I find well suited to elucidate particular themes or issues. I've included many and encourage instructors to develop their own with their students. You will find that every other paragraph or section concludes with questions I use or concepts around which I have students reflect, comparing their own lived experience in the present with an understanding of the past. These are key to my approach. Almost all instructors can search for materials, summaries, overviews, and lesson plans independently, suiting their own interests and priorities. I find, however, that when approaching a new field, my principal challenges are to know what questions are asked in the field and what debates frame the discussions, and to figure out how academic and historiographical inquiries can become everyday questions for my students. These questions—always connecting touchstones in the discipline with what students might already imagine or think about—run throughout the primer as a sort of continuous dialogue with the reader.

For example, early reconstructions and contemporary identity struggles need not be iterations of general analytic categories like "bodies," "races," or "cultures." Rather, I find that engaging teaching places subjects and points of contact in real, material contexts. So here are some ways I might enter a conversation: the history of tattooing and body art, including scarification, can be referred to and then discussed in endless variations. What do these practices mean to our students, specifically when situated within particular familial or peer relationships? Movies (even movies about pirates) feature themes that cross over maritime and Pacific histories, water sports, notably surfing (the Hawaiian sport of kings), and other forms that come down from Oceania. How do popular entertainments or recreational practices become artifacts of historical inquiry when placed back within their own times? Equally, many students know about the Pacific Ring of Fire, and illustrations of volcanic activity or, equally, world-noted archaeological splendors like Easter Island both become subjects perennially accessible for discussion. How do we get beyond stories of marvels and mysteries? Also, comparative looks at pictographs and other forms of ideographic language and representation are all ways to begin discussions without prior knowledge, which is where in most cases the teaching begins.

Think beyond the Discipline

Having explored the possibilities — there is no correct or comprehensive narration — of what Pacific histories might be, it seems appropriate to then turn to what can be organized as foundational principles and stories. I find it useful to think about putting together a teaching syllabus as analogous to other creative endeavors. My family, for a time, was in the Japanese restaurant business, and I have more than once likened teaching to preparing and serving a multicourse dinner. It takes time to conceptualize the menu and imagine the dishes, distinguish appetizers and entrees, and decide which elements go together — salty, sweet, sour, light, heavy. Actual writing and presentation I liken to creating a reduction — begin with a large pot of boiling stock and innumerable vegetables, bones, and seasonings, and evaporate them until only a fine glaze remains at the bottom — a small quantity of liquid, but intensely concentrated and flavorful.

Likewise, I encourage teachers to bring whatever experiences they carry to a teaching project. I've learned a lot from hearing my colleagues talk about their backgrounds in sports, art, dance, or business. Students come with lives: get them to think about that. For example, I have a background in music performing and recording. When I began teaching, I did not know much about writing books or lectures, but I did know how to write and make a record album. I knew we would have, say, ten tracks that constitute a complete statement or concept. Yet each track — and the sequencing is important — would do something different. One track is the lead-off tune to set a mood, one is the hit single with the catchy motif, one is the expressive ballad, and one is a piece that gets everyone up and dancing. To me, writing books and teaching plans are both this way, and so is a syllabus. The different sections do different things, even as they cohere as a complete statement of the author. Each piece has different elements or instrumentation, a rhythm, and a chorus or refrain.

INTRODUCTION

This is not such an odd way of thinking about academic teaching as it may first appear. I could make a case for insisting on the multiple ways in which histories are expressed as a function of Pacific approaches. Students should hear that the ways they understand history teaching and learning often obey a rather standard Western set of materials and practices—the archive, document, scholarly monograph, textbook, and the teacher who lectures or presents evidence, analysis, and ideas. Yet it is worth noting that Pacific Island studies, particularly, evolved and were formalized in the mid-twentieth century and so developed as a discipline in tandem with, and supported by, the approaches and methodologies of anthropologists, linguists, archaeologists, artists, storytellers, political activists, community leaders, and a wide, nonacademic imperative.

Many oral traditions have been embodied in performative approaches to teaching, and the presence of image, gesture, chant, artisanal work like carving, poetry, and other forms is readily incorporated into the academic and analytical scholarly format of other histories. It is not impossible, and in some cases not even unusual, to recognize scholars who dance, sing, chant, perform, or otherwise play out, embody, and enact histories as living principles. With proper respect and appreciation, students should understand that this is not a form of entertainment accompanying the scholarship, but a direct expression of a lived past tied to formal instruction. I encourage students to reflect upon and try to understand other examples and traditions of such embodied and enacted knowledge, and to explore ways they could express this as their own learning, drawing on their own personal histories. The caveats here are, of course, to be concerned about reckless and disrespectful cultural appropriation. No student, or teacher, should ever attempt to imitate a cultural form, practice, experience, or tradition except with honest guidance, permission, and genuine commitment. But one should ask questions and be open to learning how to learn, not regarding the unfamiliar only as other and untouchable.

One of the purposes here is to reflect on common and current conversations and debates as I understand them in Pacific histories. To approach this, I focus on placing the Pacific Islands at the center of analysis, radiating in a network to connect East Asia, Southeast Asia, the Indian Ocean, Australasia, South America, and North America in lessons, discussions, and suggested prompts, rather than focusing on continental or national histories of, for example, Japan and China, Canada, the United States, or western Latin America. Also, I highlight not the Pacific Rim, but a network across the basin. This is certainly a contested perspective, as "Pacific" has been widely and long adopted as a term to describe fundamentally East Asian histories, or North American and East Asian relations, especially in political and socioeconomic terms. In my early years of teaching Pacific histories, I was surprised how often students—and even colleagues at academic conferences—would identify my work as the study of the Pacific Rim. It seemed obvious to them that this was the proper subject of something called the Pacific. Ask students again: What is it that they understand or assume about the Pacific?

Much of this is understandable from an Occidental perspective—in Western-based teaching, the Pacific is often synonymous with war, trade, and political contests, especially between Japan, China, Taiwan, North and South Korea, and the United States, as well as European powers. I knew this geography defined many assumptions about proper subject matter and important global engagements, but felt this was not necessarily where the field should be going. Integrating those dynamics with the histories of Oceanian island peoples, Southeast Asia, and Latin America was something I wanted to do, drawing these narratives into thinking of Pacific histories as forms of world history.

I have found it useful to at least attempt to begin with what students might know about history, often a national, global, or civilizational narrative. What do they understand as the primary categories? I realized I needed to spend some time understanding how chapters in textbooks used by many students are, whether recognized or not, thematically and chronologically arranged to present theses about how time, events, and experience are organized. I had done some teaching, for example, in modern European history. Whatever themes or inflections or perspectives may be followed, generations of scholars and conventions have produced, at mini-

INTRODUCTION

mum, a debated but standard narrative: Enlightenment, French Revolution, Industrial Revolution, nationalist struggles leading up through world wars, Cold War divisions, and then on into the twenty-first century.

These are the classic, even stereotypical, textbook categories of historical writing in a particular field. Emphases and examples may underscore particular interventions — gender, race, or class questions. Yet the textbook frameworks — if only as familiar stories from which to develop counterpoints and contests — are useful. Even Atlantic history, writ large, has key markers: the Atlantic revolutions in the American colonies, France, Haiti and the Caribbean, the mercantile and slaving economies, the triangular trade, and the constant migrations and movements of peoples. Scholars have continued to explore and reexamine these. What textbook chapters and narratives are already ingrained in student thinking? Are they aware how the stories have changed over the generations?[2]

In a similar fashion, the discussions here are both synchronic and diachronic. That is, they examine relationships and connections between actors and events in a given time period, and also move sequentially across time. For this reason, the chapters do follow a general chronology — from reconstructions of ancient societies and practices up to the contemporary period. Because Pacific history as a narrative has fewer conventions than some fields, I have provided my own version of what that story might look like — from early navigations and prehistoric civilizations to atomic testing and climate change. In the last sections of the volume I am very practical, presenting references, referrals, and what I consider some helpful resources in a straightforward toolbox fashion: the exams and assignments I give, questions I ask, exercises I use, and a running account of course plans, syllabi, and digital collections (newspapers, documents, video, film, illustrations, and photographs) recommended by colleagues and contributed by teachers around the world. A good outcome for this volume would be to take away some general ideas and a few examples and then draw on the vast resources of available collections to piece together appropriate, usable, and customized teaching plans.

Before that, though, I find it useful to begin with defining terms. I recommend doing this. What do we even mean by "the Pacific"? This is some-

OBJECTIVES

thing of a fraught question in general Pacific studies, where little consensus has developed as to what might constitute an approach. Anglophone perspectives have long looked to the eighteenth century and the seminal voyages of the English navigator James Cook as foundational. Global Europeanists also focus on antecedent Spanish, Portuguese, and Dutch interventions. Asian and comparative scholars recognize Chinese and Malay political and trading networks, and Oceanian scholars emphasize the roles of island polities resulting from early migrations of peoples who would later be denominated with (and then would appropriate) some generalized identities as Pacific Islanders: Melanesians, Polynesians, and Micronesians.

These assertions, of course, seem to pose new questions: Where shall the boundaries of the Pacific be set? Should there be, in fact, many Pacifics, many domains, clustered around archipelagoes, Asian coastal empires, American maritime trading societies? Or, setting aside all but the most general of outlines framed by the continents and arbitrarily marked by the Bering Strait, the Strait of Magellan, and the Strait of Malacca, perhaps Pacific histories should be less about defining geographies than about looking at the places and points of encounter and connection, a network or constellation of shifting locales, more like wave patterns and currents rather than mapped territories.

These are daunting questions that have solid historiography behind them. Any teacher could profitably look to works by historians like Rainer Buschmann, who has designated the multiple narrations of Pacific histories, or to the great cultures and civilizations of Oskar Spate, to the microhistorical insights of Greg Dening, the global Europeanisms of Nicholas Thomas or John Gascoigne, the multisited perspectives of David Armitage and Alison Bashford, the decolonized, indigenous networks of Tracey Banivanua-Mar, or the political culture inflections of Vilsoni Hereniko.[3] But most teachers don't have time to read scores of academic studies and meet with and talk to dozens of other researchers and scholars around the world. So here I'm after a more concise overview that offers broad themes and useful examples.

Getting there can be complicated. Indeed, one of the resonant legacies of the Pacific as an academic domain is the way in which multiple specialties, journals, conferences, and scholars do not readily communicate with each other. Thus Asianists are often focused on China, Korea, and Japan and connected to Southeast Asia. South Asia is often a field apart. There is little regular communication—though there is some newer, bold scholarship—with those working in Oceanian islands (often dominated by anthropologists), and Americanists often look inwardly to the United States (though including Hawai'i and adding the Philippines), or to studies in Latin America, for political, cultural, and social coherence and geographic acceptance. What do you, or your students, think of as logically—or only tangentially—to be included?

In this way, large surveys are still appropriate. Consider single works by Shane Barter and Michael Wiener, or Dennis Flynn and Arturo Giraldez's multivolume compendia of thematic essays that survey many disciplines to describe a Pacific domain across centuries and geographies.[4] One can always begin with an overview—that is, a map and a schematic setting forth of the lands, regions, nations, and cultures to be studied. Yet one can also begin the other way around—with a particular case. This is a notable approach of Barter and Wiener, who launch their survey by focusing, for example, on a drifting, abandoned ship, years after Japan's devastating tsunami in 2011 and the way the craft transited on currents across the ocean from Japan to North America. As such, it is a figure that bears signs of histories, natural challenges, and human disaster, immediately locating the narratives of connectedness and the fluid nature of Pacific studies. Beginning with such a case—here the *Kazu Maru*—is an engaging technique that gives materiality to the larger themes. The framing here around the what, how, and why of the Pacific Basin is a good approach: one cannot speak much about something without trying to define what it is, and the Pacific is as much a construction as a subject, a point well worth elaborating.

Launching into an overview of terminologies such as the "Asia-Pacific" and the conventions of maps and geography are useful at this point. Rather than just describing regions in terms of labels, I prefer to seek out the use of those terms, those labels, and their origins. How did Polynesia become

"Polynesia?" In this way, I focus instead on the historical development of such categories and the lived experience of the Pacific; this could be also delineated as a potential attraction for readers. Often in textbooks, episodes taken from everyday life are located in sidebars. Make these sidebars, anecdotes, and examples the central ways of telling the story, launching from stories of an individual life, an immigrant tale, a boat, a note from a personal journal, a moment of conflict.

Not surprisingly, my students tend to understand the Pacific in terms of their own generation. That is, their chronological framework sets the Pacific Basin in a globalization paradigm, suggesting that the domain is of interest because of a historic shift away from an Atlantic-centered world in the late twentieth and twenty-first centuries. This is probably an indisputable claim, though it is a negative argument—the Pacific is "not" the Atlantic—and looking at maps that feature North America and Europe around the Atlantic with the Pacific divided at the Bering Strait is something of a convention that pictures the globe from an Occidental perspective. Rather, I strongly suggest that the Pacific is not suddenly becoming globalized, but is rather returning to the attention of the Atlantic world after having been advanced in navigation and voyaging, or religious and commercial power, throughout previous millennia.

In tracing out the contours of multiple cultures and civilizations, it is fine to search for common themes or purposes as linking devices, such as a coherent international-political voice, while developing from a staggering complexity of histories, cultures, and traditions. I can also appreciate the teaching approach of student friendliness here. Much classroom work can focus on the purposive energy of a scholarly *Lonely Planet* guide—rendered images of backpacking locales, historical summaries, country information, reflections on colonial legacies, and surveys of ethnic, cultural, and linguistic diversity. Offer your students material senses of places to visit and understand, foods to eat, people to meet, climates to feel. Sometimes I just bring my own collection of travel books, journals, and guides to class and read from them, which most students find engaging. We share impressions and ideas in the form of travelers' tales, relating our experiences, our understandings, and of course our misperceptions and lack of

INTRODUCTION

understanding about different parts of the world — all the more reason to want to learn the histories. Getting beyond the picturesque or touristic is key.

Though rich in detail, sights, sounds, and sketches, one thing travel guides often lack is a critical analytic framework. So, in teaching it is worth positing assertions that complex regions, such as, say, Southeast Asia, are coherent in diversity. Such claims can be framed around referencing political and international alliances such as the Association of Southeast Asian Nations, though thinking about common overlays of "mandala" political rule of local powers allied to royal houses and Buddhist cosmologies are equally important. In some cases, one can also take the almanac approach to complex regions and be more classically encyclopedic — do some prosaic but useful research starting with national surveys and statistics — with a core argument about the radiance and importance of, for example, Chinese civilization in the constitution of East Asia as a geopolitical entity. The national surveys cover the fundamentals and stand out in emphasizing the ways in which borders, boundaries, and occupations have transformed over time. This is a key point historically, of course — the map of today is only a current iteration of transformations and clashes over centuries, even millennia. Don't hesitate to compare maps across generations as evidence of this point.

Another way to show off a wider range of scholarship is, like the microhistorical case approach, to play with time by presenting histories with a thematic emphasis on memory and forgetting, a compelling lens and one that both engages the imagination and will probably be interesting for students. This approach highlights a tension not always evident in scholarship and introductory teaching: the constructedness of scholarly knowledge. One can interweave lessons that shine a light on the very parties and interests that debate and strive to control the past and present, whereas overviews will tend to hew more closely to the standard textbook approach of presenting data and standardized narratives. This approach can be notable for challenging the conventions that students call "the facts" but which are regularly debated.

Over time, I've used any number of examples for in-class debates or discussions. These have included contests like geopolitical maneuverings around the Senkaku/Diaoyu Islands between Japan and China, and how they are named and to whom they belong; or the Japanese war memorial Yasukuni (honoring war criminals or war dead?); or denials of the Rape of Nanjing legacies where commemorations are extolled or denounced. Readers can make their own analogies to other controversies. The pairing of, for example, the Japanese seizure and colonization of Manchuria with U.S. president Franklin Roosevelt's Executive Order 9066 and the internment of Japanese Americans gives specificity to the motivations of historical actors by offering comparisons as well as particular contexts. The Australian commemorations, known as Sorry Day, for historical wrongs against Aboriginal populations are also a fraught terrain. Should one apologize for the past? Can one?

All of these are profound teaching opportunities. From slavery in the United States to apartheid in South Africa to the legacies of the European Holocaust, students can certainly think of examples from their own local or national contexts. These events are contested and reinterpreted in every generation. Commemorative sites and apology debates maintain this approach to thinking about political science and history, especially, as fluid, unstable, and constantly reimagined. One hopes that other contributions to the project might reflect some of these issues; cases could be drawn from almost anywhere — Laos and Cambodia, Australia, Chile and Guatemala, coastal Canada, European states, African countries, and certainly the United States. What all of the examples above suggest is that rather than presenting the big map and picture and then trying to populate a domain, my students and I begin by assembling the picture. So, Pacific histories begin with fragments, cases, images, artifacts, and episodes. Like an interoceanic peregrination, these are assembled — it is, in fact, an assemblage approach — into this thing called Pacific histories.

PART I
Laying Foundations

Chapter One

Begin with the State of Our Knowledge

SO WE HAVE A FRAMEWORK: a field without a definitive or conventional chronology, and evidence and practices drawing upon multiple traditions, sources, and funds of evidence. Following the suggestions here, the place to begin would be at the end—in the students' contemporary period—examining cases that might relate to news or culture they already know, as in the introduction, and unfolding them historically. For the sake of narrative, however, let me follow a more conventional approach, working sequentially across time. Instructors can then begin wherever the stories and strategies meet their needs. In Pacific histories, many of the narratives come from literature, oral traditions, artifacts and archaeological traces, and linguistic, anthropological, and ethnographic evidence assembled over generations. We might think of these broadly as explorations of mythic realities and ethnographic moments.

An excellent way to teach Pacific histories, then, is to begin as they are actually practiced, as an assemblage of fragments, pieces, and conjectures about evidence, aligned with local deep times and legendary narratives. I am placing this chronologically as ancient, though of course the same approach works equally well for the contemporary period through the tools of cultural analysis and cultural studies — that is, unpacking everyday life for deeper meanings and registers of sociopolitical and cultural significance. Here, let's begin with the way one might address a traditionally prehistoric record, by transgressing upon the boundaries of archaeology and archaeologists. A number of specific cases from the Oceanic region are widely used to illustrate the likely patterns of movement and settlement in island chains.

It helps to begin with some common references. Every Pacific scholar, for example, will know some of the arguments around Lapita, an incised pottery style that is at the heart of reconstructions of an entire maritime and settlement civilization that spread from the islands of Southeast Asia down through what are today the coastal territories of Papua New Guinea, the Solomon Islands, and on toward Fiji. What can an excavated fragment or series of fragments tell us? Read a little bit about Lapita the way you would about Mayan hieroglyphics or Chinese oracle bones, inscribed forms that describe civilizations.[1] An image or artifact can show that successive populations shaped the origins of today's Polynesian peoples in narratives, drawn from an oral tradition, indicating that people voyaged long distances yet also came to be who they are exactly in the lands they now inhabit, a duality that makes sense in the context of recombining historical and ancestral temporalities.

Other examples abound: students can examine, study, and speculate on any number of artifacts and practices to think about how to historically understand ancient peoples. Some are well known and only require proper framing: you should certainly offer images of the famed moai statues of Easter Island/Rapa Nui, for example. Other examples include the transfer of the sweet potato from South America to the Oceanian realm and, for those invested in molecular biology, the broad-scale tracing of DNA lines and haplotypes from East Asia to Oceania in the work of biological and historical anthropologists like Lisa Matisoo-Smith.[2] All of this is to understand what the historiographical claim for an assemblage approach looks like in terms of actual scholarship that is used to create a mosaic of possibilities.

In my own teaching, I ask students to think about museums as places of cultural production and authority and to examine particularities of collecting and collections. Perhaps it is useful to imagine the classic cabinet of curiosities, in which early modern collectors brought together objects and items they perceived as strange, wonderful, or perplexing. How do we understand what is not initially familiar without simply looking it up, as is the habit today in the age of mobile digital technology and search engines? I immediately turn to museum collections. The visual catalogs of the Bishop Museum in Honolulu are particularly useful in this regard, though one can look to institutional collections in Fiji, Australia, New Zealand, Malaysia, Japan, China, Mexico, or other parts of the Americas.[3] From the Bishop collection in particular, somewhat familiar objects, such as tools, bowls, or tapa cloth, can be presented for discussion, and others, such as octopus lures, images of local gods, and the arrangement of heiau (sacred place) stones, are best covered in terms not only of functionality but of meaning and of investment in a spiritual and mythic universe of power and reason.

It can be useful to begin with pieces of evidence. I post or display images of an artifact, a chant, a piece of bark cloth, a canoe, or a seed crop, and ask the students to form a sense of the materiality of everyday life. First, they have to identify the meaning, purpose, and function of an artifact. The point is not to get the right answer (that's the Google reference approach) but to think critically, historically, and imaginatively, in context. As a teacher, you might choose to identify some objects, or not, or just build a larger imaginative picture based on evidence — much as researchers do themselves. A second stage would be to imagine a functioning community, to critically draw on ethnographic and historical readings or arguments to form an overall picture of what such a world encompasses.

In this regard, the noted illustrations of the famed artist of Polynesian life, Herb Kawainui Kane, are very instructive and extremely helpful, as they attempt to reveal an entire world. Kawainui Kane did considerable work for publications like *National Geographic* magazine, famed for artistic renderings and reconstructions of historical events and locales.[4] Through this, piece by piece, students are exposed to a general understanding of the cosmologies of ancient island peoples, traces and evidence, re-creating civilizations, theories of origins and migrations, the Asian heritage, and the South American question. Settlement patterns, social structure, agriculture, sustenance and trade, relations to the water world, and basic resources and materials all become part of the vision.

Examining images of individual museum pieces is always a useful way to spend time with interpreting material culture and also interrogating the very logic of museum collections themselves in terms of representative objects and artifacts and the ways that they generate carefully framed and circumscribed cultural representations out of complex histories. Early on, it is also both engaging and challenging for students to think about how to understand Pacific cultures in terms of language. Bislama and other forms of pidgin, with their overlayering of phonetic words, often from English, upon Melanesian grammars and cultural logic, can be pulled into classroom analysis and study.[5] I have at times used illustrations of signs from everyday life, and the internet can introduce more:

- Wok long rot ol kar mas stop sapos yu lukim.
- Plis no mekem shoes toti Spos yu wandem pem yu traem Or yu askem staf bifo Tonkyu long save blongyu.

I might approach the meanings of the signs above along the lines of "All cars must stop when seeing workers along the road," and "Please don't dirty the shoes. You can try them if you want them; ask the staff in advance. Thank you for your understanding." As always, languages must be treated with care and respect; to avoid caricature or false notions of understanding, such examples should only be given tentative meanings in discussion when addressed out of their own social and cultural contexts. Yet such approaches can be very useful as correctives to the idea, for example, that everyone speaks English.

Examining languages in this way can suggest common historical and cultural origins and derivatives. Austronesian languages, for example, might be examined in much the same way that students may be familiar with the Latin roots of the Romance languages, especially Spanish, French, Italian, and Portuguese. One can even try to hypothesize how geographical and temporal proximity and distance may have inflected the development of the languages, for example, Hawai'i being much farther north than the more southern and proximate Tongan and Samoan archipelagoes. I find students respond well to these challenging, but not overly taxing, nonspecialist linguistic investigations. For example:

English	island	man
Tongan	motu	tangata
Samoan	motu	tangata
Tahitian	motu	ta'ata
Maori	motu	tangata
Hawaiian	moku	kanaka
Marquesan	motu	enata

We can begin to infer groupings of similar words that may appear connected or differentiated by the distance of islands from each other. Through these fundamental discussions of material culture, archaeological evidence, and some linguistic attempts at reconstruction, we begin to formulate a few common bases to think about not only the distinctive elements of Oceanian Island cultures but also their transformations. That is, these are not only discrete pottery styles and languages in particular islands, but complicated expressions formed over time and space. They were highly mobile, and studying that mobility is a key to the next discussion.

─── *Chapter Two* ───

Secure the Fundamentals

NAVIGATION, DIASPORA, SETTLEMENT

Make Navigation a Centerpiece

Pacific histories, whether recent or of long duration, cannot be understood without invoking ancient migrations and navigation. It is useful to discuss debates from anthropology, structural and otherwise, to examine conceptions of Pacific cultures while looking at material culture such as outrigger canoes, along with considering the maritime imagination. Here, ask some apparently unanswerable questions: Did Islanders sail intentionally or not? What motivations drove them? What was the role of contingencies such as storms, and what were the signs of active navigation? Ask students how they could even begin to try and answer these questions. The point is not to have the answer, but to approach the question in terms of trying to devise a plan, an experiment, or an investigation to learn about the unknown. The common Austronesian heritage that connects Oceanic and Asian peoples together in deep time is a big idea here. This challenge requires historical thinking, but it also requires considering the recent and ever-changing revelations of archaeology and DNA science.

If we continue with the reconstruction, assemblage, and limited-knowledge inquiry approach to defining Pacific histories, the case of ancient migrations and navigations stands out because it so sharply intersects multiple questions: Where did Oceanian peoples come from? How did they get where they are? How is it possible to know? These questions are particularly resonant because they are deeply implicated in the cultural politics of Oceanian studies, and I make them a centerpiece of the first weeks of my teaching.

Early European forays into the Pacific by Spanish, Dutch, Portuguese, and later British and French explorers revealed the presence of settled island groups, but uncertainty reigned over how those settlements took place. Europeans, especially, only recently equipped with Renaissance sailing technologies, found it difficult to understand how supposedly primitive peoples could have intentionally navigated the deep-water Pacific. Speculation abounded that they had been placed where they were by God, that they were survivors of the biblical Flood or another cataclysm, or that they were survivors of shipwreck. I generally have students reflect on comparative stories, myths, and legends from around the world to understand where similarities abound among origin tales. I find that some have rich understandings of comparative traditions, but most do not, and they find the parallels enlightening.

Indeed, scholarship can be built around examining the ways that a search for origins has been reimagined across generations. The idea of reasoned, intentional sailing was disputed well into the twentieth century, and archaeology and mathematical simulations of drift currents did not resolve the issue. What is so notable is that the shift in belief came from an enacted history: a group of seafarers formed the Polynesian Voyaging Society, built a replica sailing canoe, and navigated it between Hawai'i and Tahiti with only the techniques available to ancestral wayfinders.

The story of the *Hōkūle'a* (the name of the canoe) is a necessary chapter in Pacific histories, for it draws upon the performative nature of Pacific historical thinking, is fully implicated in the politics of representation and

SECURE THE FUNDAMENTALS

cultural authority of Islanders, and has more than a little drama as the Voyaging Society attempted to find a living navigator who could guide their boat using ancient practices.[1] It is a stunning example of living history in the Pacific context, and I always teach it that way. In fact, there is much engaging teaching to do around these experimental histories, experiential histories, or in some cases reenacted histories—though the latter are generally built around an assumption that a documented event is being replicated. Still, students tend to engage well here, especially if any are themselves historical reenactors or members of the Society for Creative Anachronism, or come from backgrounds steeped in generations of ritual practices.

In the case at hand, you as the teacher should relate the story of the *Hōkūleʻa*, when a group of scholars and seafarers joined together in the 1970s to demonstrate that intentional navigation was possible by doing it themselves, thus answering critics who believed that only accidental voyaging was available to societies that were presumed to be technically primitive. Moreover, the process by which key figures such as the pilot, Nainoa Thompson, learned from the last man who still retained the traditional knowledge of celestial navigation, Mau Piailug, is a colorful and daring tale of student and master preserving an ancient form. More, Mau had to decide whether and how to share his own Micronesian traditional knowledge with navigators from other islands and different traditions. History students can surely draw upon their own knowledge to think of similar and parallel examples of when a revered, local practice is shared—or not—with others.

These important experiences of cultural pride and advocacy can also be compared to the work of adventurers and reenactors such as the Norwegian anthropologist Thor Heyerdahl, who is generally (and was for a time, famously) noted for his forays navigating a raft named *Kon-Tiki* from the coast of South America to Polynesia in an attempt to demonstrate the movement of peoples from the continent to the islands. Though his larger theory of Polynesian origins is no longer credible, these attempts to demonstrate global sailing capacities, and also the performative possibilities of history, are important for students.[2] You should find out how many of them have been involved in projects that sometimes situate participants inside a historical "experience."

A significant point of cases like the Polynesian voyaging canoes — though they are hardly the only example — is to understand that these approaches immediately underscore the critical role of mobility among Pacific peoples. Part of this is simply necessary in order to follow the historical record. The Pacific is crossed by multiple routes of migration and human colonization of territories, and archaeological and anthropological records overflow with speculation, evidence, and reconstructions of societies and civilizations driven by political and population pressures, compelled by volcanic and tidal forces to abandon earlier settlements, or — more grandly — pulled by a desire to explore.

Some of the more epic migrations we have already noted include that of the Lapita cultures from the lands that are today southern China, through Taiwan, the Philippines, and down through New Guinea and east along coastal routes to today's western and central Pacific Islands. In terms of the historical distinctions between Pacific Island cultures, it is always useful to discuss the invention and subsequent adoption of the geocultural designations of Polynesia, Micronesia, and Melanesia, denoted by the French explorer Dumont d'Urville in the nineteenth century. Examining the basic etymologies is always revealing — underscoring a European predilection for designating the many (poly-), small (micro-), and black (mela-) islands (-nesian).

The word choice stems from the perception that Melanesian islanders are phenotypically (in appearance) darker skinned, which led to assumptions about dark islands of savages. This condescension applied to all Islanders, though the distinctions are also just as instructive: Polynesians became, rather, noted as golden-toned people living idyllic lives. Thus Melanesian islands were places of barbarity, while Polynesia was paradise. The Micronesians were identified with the stereotypical tiny coral atoll and single palm tree. Noting how stereotypes about race, cultural status, naming, and immobility (isolation) operate not as absolutes but relative to other ethnically and so-called racially typed groups is instructive to students. Students often struggle over questions of race, and discussing the ways that difference is constituted in different parts of the world is worthwhile.

Establish the Foundations of Island Societies

If we argue that, historically, Pacific Island peoples were masterful navigators, intrepid voyagers, and resourceful settlement builders, why did these legacies need to be rediscovered in the twentieth century? Much of this has to do with historical conjunctures and the gradual development of the island societies themselves across centuries. In the Melanesian islands, for example, local groups divided by mountainous terrain developed what anthropologists have called Big Man cultures, well suited to forceful and charismatic rule of small domains. Patterns like this also developed initially in the islands now called Indonesia. Conversely, in the Polynesian islands, resources drawn both from the sea and from the effective use of sedentary agriculture led to highly ritualized hierarchical societies, with nobles, commoners, and warrior and priestly groups. It is important here to devote time to examining survival systems and exchange networks—the everyday life of historical actors.

Teaching this is always fascinating because it can be so usefully compared to other political systems (especially European and Asian) that are stratified in social orders based on kinship, royal families, and bloodlines to the present day. Students can work with these issues through role-plays. I randomly organize students into teams representing island groups and give them cards or markers listing a variety of sociopolitical organizations and available resources. There are cards for strong warrior clans, access to abundant fishing stocks, protection of a powerful spiritual site, or kinship ties in other islands. The groups are encouraged to consider trading cards as a practice of exchange, and to consider intermarriage with other groups in order to ensure their own stability and growth. The cultures need not be denominated specifically (that would require extensive actual knowledge), but an understanding of the fundamental dynamics is always engaging, especially since the resources are intentionally unevenly distributed. Some groups find they must try to forge alliances, while others are in a position to exert authority. Students find it all inherently complicated.

We then compare this to what we know of the historical record. As much as they developed in different archipelagoes, Islander societies also involuted—that is, they became largely self-sustaining within their own terrains—and political energy went toward leadership struggles, local challenges for paramount status, and the pedigrees created by kinship ties through great family alliances. The Pomare in Tahiti and the Kamehameha lines in Hawaiʻi come to mind. A key effect of this is that the Islander societies entered a historic phase no longer devoted to long-distance migration, but to population growth and resource intensification in newly identified home territories.[3] Students should definitely think about how familial ties affect and even define politics worldwide and across history, whether dynastically through monarchies and aristocracies or by blood and intermarriage—even in democratic republics. Having elected politicians does not prevent most countries from paying special attention to family dynasties of relatives, spouses, and sons and daughters. U.S. students may think of the Kennedy family. In India, the Nehru-Gandhi family comes quickly to mind. What are some other obvious examples to students—particularly in Europe, Asia, or the Middle East?

Historically, the gradual self-sufficiency of island cultures was widely noted by outlanders, such as European explorers, as enabling the isolation of the Islanders, even though the heritage and ties of a tremendously networked Oceania were at hand. The critical moment of isolation actually occurred during the Western colonial era, largely in the nineteenth century, when imperial boundaries were drawn and movements, often along traditional routes, were interdicted in defense of European colonial territories. A notable teaching moment here is to consider examples where a quality like isolation might describe not an existential state—that is, a particular people who are small in number and geographically distant from others—but a condition generated by political forces. Think about how states generate their own borders, territories, zones, walls, and spheres of influence to claim their own experiences of security and exclusion. Students are generally good at understanding the idea of protecting borders and boundaries of a home territory when such concerns arise. Do they understand how this separation can also be imposed on others?

In this context it is also worthwhile to note that Pacific Island societies developed their own regional empires or at least political and commercial alliances, so that even while developing internally, they yet maintained networks across their adjacent seas. An early civilization in Pohnpei drew peoples from around today's Micronesian islands and established a capital of formidable stone structures that have left stunning ruins. In the same part of the Pacific, the high island of Yap held sway over low-lying tributaries across atolls and reef societies, and in Tonga, canoe fleets reached out to Samoa and maintained a respected, and at times feared, royal household. In a related vein, off the eastern tip of New Guinea, Trobriand Islanders have long been famed for their heavily ritualized Kula rings of exchanging goods and symbolic shell bracelets and armbands, describing a society of mobility and constant reinforcement of widely flung contacts and relationships.[4] Students should think about how to understand the roles of gift giving, trade, buying and selling, and instrumental exchange, and how they operate differently. Ask them: Why does one offer gifts and in what context? What is a gift? What kind of obligations or recognitions are entailed?

For students who are interested in other aspects of exchange, value, and the personal dynamics of economics, Islander culture studies provide an entry into a fascinating debate on the natural condition of the human species. In classic studies of Western civilization, these arguments can be derived from the works of Thomas Hobbes, John Locke, and Jean-Jacques Rousseau and can be framed around the question of scarcity. Pacific Islands, interestingly, are often examples in historical and thought experiments that serve as models of a larger world, and I recommend spending some time pursuing these. One approach depicts Pacific islands as barren rocks, desert islands full of savages, a land of castaways and shipwrecks, faraway and treacherous places to be lost and alone. Equally, the paradise stereotype is endemic in the Polynesian Pacific islands, with its evocations of beaches, sun, and palms, but also abundant fish and fruit and the promise of a life without work. This imaginary was fueled by early reports about Tahiti by French navigators like Bougainville and intertwined with fantasies of supposedly uninhibited female eroticism, an Eden combining both pleasure and the endless bounty of Nature. It would be easy to present such images for students by drawing upon modern travel and tourist literature. Offer examples.

This narrative has persisted into the present. It manifested in the twentieth century with utopian projects to settle colonies in the South Seas to escape the perils of modernity, and was given a globally popular rendering by the anthropologist Margaret Mead in the classic *Coming of Age in Samoa*, from which general readers seemed to take away the singular notion that Samoan girls were not emotionally or psychologically conflicted about their personal pleasures concerning lovemaking or growing up. On the other hand, scholars such as Jared Diamond have drawn on the story of Rapa Nui/Easter Island to suggest how reckless resource extraction and depletion of a fragile ecosystem (a cautionary tale) can lead to desperate scarcity, the inability to support a growing population, and even the collapse of a civilization.[5]

I work with both of these ideas, having students read passages from Mead while pondering the languorous presentation of simple lives, and also encouraging students to understand material limits drawn from ecological science. Any number of students are always interested in environmental studies and questions of sustainability. We have discussions about how often island environments are taken as laboratories, or isolated testing grounds for all sorts of philosophical, scientific, or human experiments. Can students cite their own examples from literature or popular culture where the island has become a figure for organizing an ideal society or has become the location of a sinister mystery or lost civilization?

Chapter Three

Underscore the Connections

ENCOUNTERS IN THE CONTACT ZONE

Understand the Asian Heritage

In teaching histories of the Pacific world, my preference is to begin with the ocean domains—that is, the Pacific Islands, as they tend to be the most overlooked in general surveys that favor a Pacific Rim approach to the study of the region, with strong emphasis on Asia and the Americas. Focusing on the islands from the beginning highlights what some scholars regard as archipelagic cultures and their particular features, being bounded and defined by oceans, seas, and connected yet discontinuous territories. Such studies also define regions like the Caribbean and parts of the Indian Ocean. To a certain degree this was also true of classic Mediterranean studies such as those by historian Fernand Braudel—rather than focusing on nations on land, look to the sea as a culture and connector in itself for the rise of civilization. In fact, this is often a good time to study a world map and recognize that the Pacific is globalized and heavily impacted by currents and cultures coming out of the Indian Ocean, which ties together the African continent and Middle East to Oceania.

Where an Occidental vision of geography places the Pacific between Asia and the Americas, a Pacific orientation requires a basic introduction of Arabic and Indian influences through key places of flow and transit, such as the Strait of Melaka, commonly known as Malacca. I recommend taking some time to focus on such usually unfamiliar places. Attention to local powers is a splendid way to understand how maritime worlds work by control of strategic waterways. Here, students will see how authority derives from the control of sea traffic and the movement of sailors, traders, teachers, goods, and ideas. One can think of many examples in world history. Students can reflect on the importance of the Panama and Suez canals, for example, or naval control of the Persian Gulf, or contemporary controversies about sovereignty and national waters involving China, a wide range of Southeast Asian nations including the Philippines and Vietnam, and the United States.

Historically, control of waterways like the Strait of Melaka defined power and policy, including the coastal domains ruled by sultans and island-based archipelagic states such as an ancient civilization called Srivijaya, in what is today Indonesia. Connections of trade and faith through the islands of Southeast Asia and the waterways of Indonesia, Irian Jaya, and Papua New Guinea are also critical. Well worth noting here is that the local rulers in these islands took the titles of sultan, rajah, and datu. Their influences came very much from South Asia and the Indian subcontinent.

Teachers wishing to tie in continental histories of ancient China can frame chronologies that focus on the Shang rulers (about 2000 BCE), famed for their oracle bone inscription writing and the efflorescence of agriculture and population. A good marker is the flourishing age of classical Chinese technologies and philosophy in the sixth century BCE, including the teachings of Confucius. On the Indian subcontinent, the same century would note the continuing formalization of the caste system and the birth and dissemination of the works of Siddhartha Guatama, the Buddha. Through traders, teachers, navigators, and migrants, Pacific cultures drew knowledge, including cosmologies, from Hindu and Indian

Buddhist traditions. This was particularly resonant in Southeast Asia, in today's Malaysia and Indonesia, and it has become conventional in history writing to think of the local polities not in terms of a center and periphery, or a state, but as a mandala system — overlapping and interconnecting rings of authority and dependence within a spiritual cosmology. These histories can be understood in terms of potentates and peers, finely balanced political authorities in constant tension.

For visuals that will capture both the cosmologies and grandeur of these civilizations (like Srivijaya), you should definitely draw on images of Borobudur, a Buddhist temple complex on the island of Java in Indonesia. There, pilgrims trace the life of the Buddha by walking around and up its concentric stone terraces to reach the full expression of emptiness at the summit. Students should be encouraged to think about historical worlds as living worlds, and to understand what they are learning both from instruction and also as travelers, explorers, and *Lonely Planet*-type trekkers themselves. They should be ready to discuss what they are learning about the history of locales with which they may be unfamiliar, but also to think about imagined (or real) travels, where they will stay, what they will eat, how they will get from one place to another, and who they will need to know and what to say and observe. Perhaps students can keep their own travel logs or diaries as an exercise.

To capture the world of the sultans, I have often spent a bit of time on Melaka (Malacca) because it is an excellent example of a port that flourished as a result of what today would be considered international commerce. The history is legendary and fascinating — a pirate prince (Parameswara, later rechristened Shah Iskandar) who founds a colony and soon gains wealth and power by controlling the local strait. Moreover, it incorporates multiple elements that are historically rich. The waters were patrolled by sea people known as the *orang laut* (*orang* meaning a person, and *laut* the sea). Students may pick up on one of the most familiar Malay words, *orangutan*, which refers to the great ape as a person of the forest. The sea people served as a sort of naval force and protection fleet, compelling ships passing by to trade locally. Critically, the passing ships were transiting between the Indian Ocean and the South China Sea, and ultimately the Pacific, so Melaka was in many ways the gateway between the oceans and also between east and west.[1] In fact, it is located in the region where monsoon winds shifted back and forth seasonally. Students can reflect on how much geography and natural forces can shape the fortunes of polities and peoples.

This was also true in the archipelago that would become the Philippines, with local settlements and cultures developing around communities called the *barangay*, whose leaders took titles that reflected Southeast Asian aristocracy, and with religious faiths drawing on Islam and local practices. The role of faith is a critical study here, for students can often be surprised to learn that the largest Muslim population is not in the Middle East but in Indonesia. Together with Malaysia, Brunei, and the southern islands of the Philippines, it is Asia and the Pacific that host the most diverse and historic Islamic cultures. Does this at all shape students' understanding of global Islam?

Into this world of local rulers and connected communities came an even greater force of exploration and authority, demanding recognition and tribute. When it comes to fortunes and power on a grand scale, this is an open invitation to engage with one of the staples of global history: the Chinese Treasure Fleets under the command of the admiral Zheng He. If you teach world history, then you already certainly study the Treasure Fleets. They were composed of scores of ships and boats, navigating from coastal China to Japan, through Melaka and across the Indian Ocean as far as the Arabian Peninsula and, by reliable records, all the way down the African coastline near Madagascar. For a generation after 1400, this was indeed an era when China ruled the seas. The staggering size, scope, and voyaging scale of the Treasure Fleets is particularly interesting, first, because scholarship about them has framed new narratives about maritime exploration from Asia to contest the much more familiar narratives of Europeans like Ferdinand Magellan, Vasco da Gama, and Christopher Columbus. This is a good time to ask students about which explorers and navigators are globally famous.[2] Why are some feats so well known, and others less so? Who decides which histories are told, and how does this change over time?

UNDERSCORE THE CONNECTIONS

For maritime aficionados, the fleets themselves offer a great deal to study—they have been rightly likened to floating cities, equipped with war vessels, cargo ships, stables, kitchens, gardens, savants, soldiers, and traders, everything that an entire community might need for sea voyages extending over years. It is worthwhile noting how evidence points to Chinese fleets sailing as far as the East African coastline, and one can always make good use of how the unknown becomes understood, as when the fleet brought back a giraffe to the Ming emperor, and the ways that the court likened it to a magical Quilin animal, thereby fitting into an East Asian worldview. The admiral, Zheng He, is himself always worth study. He was, famously, a Muslim, taken as a captive from a territory that was only marginally Chinese in his era, and he rose through ability in the emperor's court system. He is often cited, correctly, as a truly intercultural figure. Recognizing that such mixed identities were common enough in a prenational era is always valuable. His presence also allows a further interrogation of the significance of Islam in the Pacific world. Students often find it compelling to interpret what they might already know about: legends of the silk and spice routes through Central Asia to China, Arab traders and mariners coming out of the Arabian peninsula and sailing across the Indian Ocean.

Students often know tales of legendary figures like Sinbad the Sailor, with his fantastical adventures, drawn from these traditions. In fact, so many students currently are steeped in commercial movies and tales drawing on literary and legendary traditions that an entire discussion can be built around them. Which elements are historically recognizable in terms of personages, locations, and worldviews? Which are wholly fantastical or built up? A great deal of scholarship, for example, has gone into tracing particular Sinbad tales to Sri Lanka (Ceylon) as a fabled land of treasure, or considering the orangutans of Indonesia as models for great beasts that terrified men.

Most knowledge of the Treasure Fleets was forgotten for centuries, and recovering that knowledge coincided with contemporary interest in China as a rising power by the late twentieth century.[3] Successive modern governments after Deng Xiaoping took interest in representing

China as maritime and global, rather than as an insular agrarian nation. Most broadly, discussions of the Treasure Fleets make clear that China is hardly a new rising power at all; in many ways, it is simply returning to a dominance in East Asian affairs and global influence that is part of its thousands of years of history, only briefly interrupted by the legacies of nineteenth-century colonialism and internecine communist and nationalist struggles in the twentieth.

How current geopolitics and memories constantly reshape the historical record runs all through this story. Historically, the Treasure Fleets are critical because they show how China could assert power and tributary authority without conquest, but also because they were keenly interested in commercial possibilities and — perhaps most important — they left behind colonies of Chinese settlers who jumped ship, established offices and intimate relations with locals, and built new, diasporic communities around the known world. The ways that all voyages, conquests, trade, or explorations on any large scale result in the establishment of settlements, intimate relationships, and new culturally and ethnically mixed groups is an important historical lesson.

Introduce the Europeans

At a certain point in teaching about the Pacific, it is important to introduce Westerners into the story. These are the outlanders coming into Asia. Broadly, this would mean explorations, encounters, and contacts with, especially, voyaging parties from Portugal, Spain, and the Netherlands. At this juncture, you should take advantage of the moment to note how much history — if one follows this more or less chronologically — has been told without Europeans. It may be worthwhile to note that Anglophile accounts of the Pacific often begin with the voyages of navigator James Cook in the eighteenth century, and Iberian chronicles will push that back to Ferdinand Magellan in the sixteenth. In fact, Magellan did give the body of water he traversed the name by which it is globally known today (El Mar Pacifico) based on his impression that the great ocean was placid. However, an overview should always note how much Austronesian migrations, Polynesian navigation and settlement, and principalities and civilizations built through the Malay world with influences from the Indian Ocean predated the Europeans. The role of China as a dominant power, the impact of Buddhism and Islam, and sophisticated genealogies of gods, deities, demigods, and local spirits are key historical elements across the islands and mainland shores by the turn of the fifteenth century. Westerners came later.

How then might you tell the story of Europeans? Though narrated in Western histories as exploits of daring navigation and discovery, it is important to recognize that these framings—perhaps correct—betray a certain historic perspective. It is equally true to say that, even from a European perspective, what was daring was to rely on Arab navigators in the Indian Ocean (as Vasco da Gama did) or to rely on previous knowledge of Southeast Asian waters gained from colonial exploits (which Magellan did). In both cases, the Portuguese and Spanish navigators used local pilots and guides and were heading into waters unknown only to them. They were entering a world of civilizations millennia old, with highly sophisticated political, trading, and spiritual cultures. It is worth noting that wealthy Asian states were rich in ivory, gold, spices, silks, and hardwoods, while Europeans managed only woolens and simple manufactures. Thus, it is important to ask students if they see that current scholarship has focused on exploration and especially encounter, and moved decisively away from discovery as a way of describing the exploits of European navigators and voyagers.

This is a great point at which to engage students again with cartography—that is, not maps of the regions studied so they can orient themselves, but historical maps indicating not just spatial understanding but entire religious worldviews. You should compare medieval illustrations, representing the world organized around the necessary focal point of the Garden of Eden, often with Adam and Eve and the serpent, and waters that course around a world defined by Christendom. Equally, Renaissance maps often show the shapes of the continents and oceans as we know them today, yet also have features that are to our eyes anachronistic: the population of the blank spaces with allegorical figures, representations of peoples who were only imagined, and, most critically, geographical features that are nonexistent.

Perhaps most significant is the Terra Australis Incognita, which modern observers often equate, reflexively, with Antarctica. But on early maps, it is, in fact, the Great Southern Continent of legend, the last undiscovered part of the world, wherein might reside wealth and splendor to rival those of the kingdoms encountered by the Spanish in the New World, and where legendary kings, saints, and monsters dwelled—having been found nowhere else in the known world. Students can pay attention to one of the most intriguing aspects of historical cartography: many features were included because of assumptions drawn from tradition and belief, rather than observation.[4] For students interested in historical geographies or speculative fiction, how have imaginary landscapes of realms, domains, kingdoms, or hidden lands shaped their imaginations?

It is always instructive to think about how mapping, space, and place are manifested for students in their own experiences: Where do they imagine are the places unknown, and with what boundaries and means of access? It is worth noting that the paradigmatic Enlightenment navigator, James Cook, was in part sent on his first world-encircling mission precisely to find, or at least determine, the reality of the Great Southern Continent for the British navy. It is a truthful generalization that his fame rests upon discovery of things unknown to Europeans but also upon demythifying and disproving things that were not true, such as the existence of the Southern Continent and, in his time, the Northwest Passage over the top of the world between the oceans (in the twenty-first century, climate change has altered the reality of this, interestingly enough).

These forays were marked by encounter, negotiation, and accommodation. Later political organization and industrial power by which European forces overpowered local kingdoms is broadly a phenomenon of the nineteenth century, not the fifteenth or, really, the eighteenth. There were, of course, notable contests—such as that of the Portuguese in Melaka, Macao, and throughout the Indonesian islands. Still, these conquests were footholds only—strongholds and outposts, jealously guarded and insular within the surrounding power of other Asian polities.⁵ Some, like Macao, were retained at the indulgence of imperial Chinese authority, and other ports like Melaka in fact changed hands multiple times over generations.

A similar experience of the constantly shifting nature of power in maritime Asia also characterized later interlopers into the Indonesian islands — the Dutch, beginning with small parties, very much strangers and of little interest to the local authorities. The organization of the Dutch East India Company, the famed VOC (by its Dutch initials), changed all this, and is a fascinating figure around which to organize discussions. I strongly recommend you teach a little about the VOC because, first, it was established under a charter that resembles a joint-stock company with shareholders. I discuss this in terms of modern financial institutions and engage students with an interest in business, who will find all of their subjects engaged here: finance, accounting, management, marketing, and — especially — supply chains. You'll probably have students who find combinations of history and business to be novel.

Second, the VOC was charged with the authority to obtain its own ships, contracts, and — especially — military forces. Students can reflect on the meaning of a state within a state or, more to the point, an organization that is a state unto itself. Third, it was arguably the world's first multinational corporation, operating through capital investment all around the world from the Netherlands to Southeast Asia. Fourth, it is the most famous historical example of an organization trying to corner the market for particular, rare, natural products that become commodities; in this case, spices. You can always make analogies to current controlled substances, especially among pharmaceuticals, data mining information, or cryptocurrencies as movers of tremendous wealth. What power can current multinational corporations exert over markets, capital, and politics?

The discussion of spices opens up a whole set of teaching possibilities: the botany and environmental context of cloves and nutmeg, which grew nowhere else in the world except in the Spice Islands; the market forces that sent fleets of traders and warships to conquer and control tiny islands on the other side of the world for the sole purpose of acquiring a valuable plant product; the early modern imagination of islands where grew trees that provided such immense wealth that it was as if they sprouted money; and the local populations that were murdered in order to control the trees. Perhaps most important of all is the historical lesson of transformation over time: how a seed for which tens of thousands died, and fortunes were made and lost, is today sold in grocery stores for a few dollars. It is also important to note that the spice routes, like the Silk Road, were of ancient provenance, and indicative of long-standing trade between maritime Southeast Asia, China, Central Asia, and Europe. Corridors of the world were globalized long before the modern era of declared cultural and commercial globalization.

Spices are easy to engage students with materially: I make a simple trip to a grocer to acquire a small packet or bottle of cloves, nutmeg, or cinnamon. Most can be had for a very small cost (or borrowed from one's own kitchen) and can become the centerpiece of discussions: How much would students pay for a few ounces? Can they imagine becoming fabulously wealthy by collecting the stuff of corner market spice racks today? How is it possible to imagine fleets willing to conquer and murder to obtain a kitchen commodity? If all of this seems impossible, think of contemporary elements of international and illegal drug trading, and how syndicates and cartels include violence in their methods of controlling the market for botanical substances like cocaine and its derivatives. What allows—even encourages—such enterprises to flourish? What kinds of organization and structure are needed, from harvest to distribution?

Define the Spanish Lake

This is a good moment for you to frame a geographic context for these stories. How strongly conquest and treasure motivated exploration would likely be evident to any student of Spanish history—especially as it impacted the histories of the New World—the Americas. The Americas, obviously, form the eastern continental frame to the Pacific region. Scholarship, especially in archaeology and anthropology, has traced the eminence of the Aztec and Inca empires in contemporary Mexico and Peru and, in the latter case, the legendary tradition of gods leaving the mainland and heading out over the waters of the Pacific. The gradual imposition of Spanish authority across much of Central and South America meant that Spanish impact in the Pacific was, existentially, as much a product of the Americas as of Spain in Europe.

Moreover, understanding the Pacific through a Spanish imperial lens indicates that its distance from Europe was not predominant in Spanish thinking—rather, the Pacific was an extension of empire in the Americas, giving them a legal and historical claim on what would become known as the Spanish Lake, a term for the network of ports and trade that crisscrossed between the Philippines, Mexico, and Peru.

Voyages by the likes of Álvaro de Mendaña and Pedro Fernández de Quirós launched from the viceroyalty of Peru, and the great trading ports for the Spanish were at Monterey in today's California and at Acapulco in what became Mexico. Have students reflect on the fact that the Portuguese sailed to Asia and the Pacific around the African continent and across the Indian Ocean, while the Spanish crossed the Atlantic and entered the Pacific through their colonies in the Americas. Part of this was a function of the Treaty of Tordesillas, which established that to conquer and claim new territory, the Portuguese must sail east from Europe and the Spanish west. As the earth is a sphere, they were bound to meet in the Pacific in Asia.

As the historian Rainer Buschmann notes, the main framework begins with a challenging assertion: ventures into the Spanish Lake were only partly about mastering the Pacific. Rather, they were parts of global claims and colonies whereby Spain—which touches the Pacific not at all—extended itself to distant territories through empire in the Americas and created a continuous linkage through the galleon trade from New Spain (Mexico) to the Philippines. Indeed, as with the modern change in scholarship to understand that Europeans did not really "discover" other peoples and lands (except for themselves), Spanish explorations were not really ventures into a new world but an extension of a known empire in the Americas.[6]

In thinking of history through the lens of empire, then, a key point is to understand early on that global empire was, if not exactly a fiction, certainly a contingent and ever-shifting array of strong and weak emplacements and outposts, circulations of labor and administrators, traders, and missionaries, highly dependent on local populations. It is not surprising that the Spanish Empire in the Pacific was as much accidental and opportunistic as part of a grand design, and also significantly imaginary and unsustainable. Can the students think of other examples where an institution (be it a system of rule, a political body, or an extended community) is really just the sum of its parts?

To underscore this, instructors should take care to emphasize the reality of empires and their subjects. For example, in this case it is critical to extensively underscore the key role of non-Spanish actors in the shaping of the Spanish Lake. Notable are the Chinese mestizos who built up and defended the Philippines, with reference to the complex, comparative racial typologies employed in the islands and the tenuous alliances, rivalries, and conflicts between the different communities. The Philippines, rather than being truly Spanish, were rather a locale where Malay, Micronesian, Chinese, indigenous, and mixed-blood peoples took on Spanish customs and practices, constantly negotiating for social status and political power. Try illustrating this through individual character portraits and reconstructions of interesting groups, such as the Real Principe Chinese mestizo regiment during the Seven Years' War. Also, encourage students to think about how different institutions — such as military, academic, and social clubs and fraternal organizations, or political parties — advance their own members over time and what kind of tensions these examples of favoritism create. Why do some members of a society go to particular schools, meet in particular clubs, and sometimes exclude others? How are insider and outsider defined?

The idea that the Spanish controlled some sort of imperial domain was contested, especially with the arrival of the British and French, and a shift occurred, away from the Pacific as a place of Spanish rule and treasure, to one — in an eighteenth-century Enlightenment era — of science, exploration, and self-discovery. The evolving narratives about identity, civilization, nationalist history, subjectivity, and social status can be developed through figures both well and lesser known in concurrent and successive debate: Álvaro de Mendaña and Pedro Fernández de Quirós, Diego Luis de San Vitores, Alexander von Humboldt, Alejandro Malaspina, and a host of others. A little old-fashioned great-men biography can also be occasionally useful and instructive.

A good part of the historical story comes down to who writes it. Spanish intellectuals were ever present yet regrettably never as prolific as other Europeans in publishing accounts, allowing significant Spanish accomplishments to be overshadowed by a Black Legend interpretation of cruelty and Inquisition that for so long submerged Spanish historiography about the Pacific. These narratives were also abetted by British historians writing about Spanish weaknesses around the Seven Years' War, when Manila was occupied by the British, and the fairly complete humiliation of the 1898 Spanish-American War, extending a broader pattern of colonial fragmentation already long unrolling in the Americas. Don't miss a chance to discuss what today might be called revisionism, spin, or the story of the victors. How much is the history we know determined by who controls the message? How close can one get to the truth of past events and experiences?

Through political and military chronicles, the social and cultural chronicles of new populations emerge to frame a Hispanized rather than strictly Spanish history of the Pacific. In fact, it was not only Spain but a direct rivalry between Spain and Portugal that truly frames one of the signal moments in Oceanian history: the European transit and naming of the Pacific by the globally renowned Ferdinand de Magellan, the first known circumnavigator of the world and first European to cross the Pacific from east to west — naming the ocean itself in due course. The legend of Magellan's travels is interesting for students in that he has been portrayed as a bold, and perhaps reckless, explorer and discoverer of unknown worlds. The record, however, is actually more interesting. Magellan knew very much where he wanted to go from Europe, having spent years in colonial military service with the Portuguese in maritime Southeast Asia. When he proposed his mission to the Spanish Crown (who had presumed title to lands Europeans discovered by sailing west), he was sailing not into the unknown, but toward the spice strongholds of the Portuguese.

In a prenational era, he was bound to royal favor, not countries, and his navigator was a slave he had acquired during a siege of Melaka (Malacca), Enrique. It was Enrique, as a native guide and navigator, who provided much of the voyaging knowledge credited to Magellan and his party. In focusing on the transpacific voyage, challenge students with any number of larger questions. Somewhat analogous to the now-disputed legacies of Christopher Columbus, to what degree were great explorers as heroic as often portrayed? In what ways were they men of their time? How many of their accomplishments were due not to individual courage and genius, but to active collaboration with local informants, navigators, and agents?

What is the role of local and regional informants in shaping historical events—while they themselves disappeared from the record? What did Magellan encounter when he sailed from the southern tip of South America to the Philippines? Upon landfall in today's Philippines, Magellan was met by Rajah Humabon, wealthy through trade with Southeast Asia. Humabon and his people agreed to convert to Catholicism and requested that Magellan take on a rival chieftan, Lapu Lapu, on an adjoining island. The result is that an overconfident Magellan was slain on the beach, an event—in some quarters—celebrated as the first armed resistance to a colonialist foreign invader.[7] This is always an intriguing lesson on who is denominated a historical or national hero, and how this is highly dependent on not only context, but generation. Have students reflect on how commemoration, rehabilitation, revisionism, memory, and historical dispute all contribute to lively, continuing debates about how heroes are made or manufactured and for what ends. Why do some figures have statues and not others? Why are monuments sometimes taken down?

Connect the Japanese World of the Samurai

Depending upon your interests, you can focus on developing the Spanish Pacific or, geographically, frame those stories at the other extreme by looking to the Asian Pacific. One of the places for a classic East-meets-West narrative—combining analyses of contact, encounter, uneasy accommodation, and ultimately mutual exploitation and benefit—is the Japan of the sixteenth century. This was an age of samurai and pirates, alliances and contests. This is always an intriguing case study that can underscore how a small cohort of foreigners—in this case Portuguese Jesuit priests—could have an extraordinary impact on another people. The Christian Century in southern Japan can be told through the port of Nagasaki, where Jesuits and traders landed, partly in search of the fabled island kingdom of Cipangu, which they knew to exist off of the Chinese coast—and which turned out to be Japan.

The Japanese had a hierarchical and highly sophisticated social order, led by great aristocratic families and clans and supported by the famed warrior class, the samurai. Have students pull references from many avenues of popular culture to describe and discuss the order and the look of this feudal society. Generally, some students are fanciers of samurai warrior culture, or are fascinated by the stylings of art and culture. Of course, more than a few will be steeped in the global phenomena of anime and manga, the Japanese animated and graphic-comic series that have reshaped so much of popular culture. It would be surprising if you did not have at least a few experts among your students. Draw on their interest.

The Christian tale is a good example not of overwhelming Western power—as it would be in the nineteenth century—but of small parties gaining leverage within a fragmented political system. At the time the Portuguese landed, Japan was in the throes of a generations-long civil war, with constantly shifting alliances and small advantages bringing victories in the field. The lord of Nagasaki was overshadowed by more powerful neighbors but found the Jesuits useful: they brought Western weapons, the promise of help from an outside ally, and a militant Jesuit faith that challenged the authority of the local Buddhist monasteries, which were often rival political centers.[8] Ask students if they understand how religious orders were often very powerful materially and not just spiritually—and could be trained militarily, as with the famous warrior-priests.

The Jesuits achieved their aims of acquiring Japanese converts and local authority, and the Japanese lords were able to align themselves with new forms of power and authority. Do encourage your students to examine the ways that religion and politics often overlap and are useful to each other, especially in tenuous situations. By contrast, Christians were persecuted and expelled by the seventeenth century—at a time when the civil wars ended and the shoguns, military rulers, once again imposed central authority over Japan: the Jesuits were suddenly no longer needed and themselves posed a rival threat. Solid lessons can be gained about changing fortunes and reading them correctly.

Explore the Fascination of Pirates

Another subject of perennial fascination to students that also engages the themes of political alliances and contests framed by tumultuous politics is the phenomenon of piracy. The world and history of pirates never cease to intrigue, framed as they are by depictions in popular culture, contemporary challenges, and a sociology that tacks between international criminality and desperate livelihoods. The romance of pirates and piracy is a constant in popular culture, from literature to film, and students can undoubtedly provide many examples and references, including the *Pirates of the Caribbean* extravaganzas. Similarly, piracy is a powerful lens through which to understand economic disruption, social upheaval, and the boundaries between lives chosen and determined.

Pirate narratives still feature prominently off the coast of Somalia, in the South China Sea, and along disputed waterways worldwide where maritime policing is weak or impractical. Chinese, Japanese, and Malay pirate bands were all familiar in the early modern Pacific, particularly along the Chinese coast and throughout the archipelagoes of the South China Seas, where rings of islands, coves, bays, and unknown passages provided the proverbial hidden bases and ports for many pirates. The literature is dotted with colorful figures, often partly legendary: Limahong, Lady Ching, Koxinga—brilliant strategists who ruled over their own pirate states and challenged governments for treasure, tribute, and authority over the seas. Their backgrounds were also widely varied: disgraced royalty at war within a family; petty criminals rising to eminence; savvy operators working their way up inside a system.

Have students discuss and debate why pirate clans and societies form. Who are pirates? Move them toward pondering and learning that most pirate groups were not colorful bands but legions of the dispossessed—

peasants pushed off lands into coastal poverty and thieving, local traders and sellers forced outside the law by colonial monopolies imposed on their traditional businesses.[9] The question of what makes a pirate, or what boundaries or laws can suddenly criminalize the practices of entire communities, is always an important debate.

It is, at the same time, equally well to note that pirates were not only challengers to imperial states but were also feared by villagers across the Pacific and regularly associated with slavers who swept into largely defenseless settlements looking for laborers to take captive and sell in other islands. Piracy has evolved from early modern bands terrorizing local settlements to highly organized criminal gangs, still kidnapping and ransoming, or looting and stealing cargoes along highly trafficked waterways around the world. Are students familiar with pirate news from today's South China Sea, Strait of Melaka, or Philippine archipelago? What do they share in common?

—— *Chapter Four* ——

Review Disputed Legacies and Arguments

Think of World Systems

One of the ways to draw together multiple historical questions—where pirates come from, how empires define their boundaries, the degree to which the Pacific has been isolated, the globalization of the world in the twenty-first century—is to think of how apparently disparate themes and cases can be articulated around a single cogent example. For the above, a classic means would be to examine the intriguing and long-lasting phenomenon of the Spanish galleon trade, which pulled together the cultures and politics of Asia and the Americas. This overlaps maritime, political, cultural, and economic histories and is an exemplar of a broad thesis that you will find it critical to discuss with students: that globalization, understood as an active exchange of goods, information, labor, and cultural forms with impacts unbounded by geography, has long political and historical antecedents in the Pacific.

Naturally, reference can be made to other long-distance commercial chains of wealth and power—the ancient silk and spice routes from Europe to Asia and back, over both land and sea. The galleon trade, a regular cycle of fabulously wealthy treasure ships sent into a closely guarded circuit, or *volta*, of winds from Manila to Acapulco, is fascinating. Manila was the entrepôt for luxuries coming from all across Asia, particularly China, and Acapulco was the site of the Spanish viceroyalty. The story of the goods received and the dangers involved in sending them (e.g., storms and shipwreck, pirates, unscrupulous agents, changing demand and fashions) will engage students with any interests in business, supply chains, and risk management. The galleon trade is an example of high-stakes and high-reward investing, and entire communities could stake their fortunes on a successful venture. It is also a tale of local communities of shipbuilders in Manila and Mexico, shops, provisioners, and an entire infrastructure of services and businesses that grow up around a major enterprise.[1] This is an excellent moment for you to challenge students to think of how one huge business in a region can come to dominate — and perhaps control — an entire economy.

Moreover, the galleons did not simply sail directly from port to port — that was impossible in this era — but with the winds: through the Pacific Islands, particularly Guam, and along the California coastline, connecting continents and island chains, encountering and engaging with local indigenous and Native American populations. Such trade through and with China also meant that silver coinage was shipped from the New World to Asia. Much of the silver came from Indian slave labor in Peru and in Mexico, tying the colonial history of labor exploitation to the international goods trade. You can use maps to demonstrate the interconnected flow of materials and interests over a stunningly large geography long before modern transportation and communication networks and systems.

The galleons are interesting because of their cultural impact. Bringing in silks and luxury wares from Asia shaped both aristocratic and popular tastes in New Spain (Mexico), setting standards for, in some cases, hybrid local fashion statements. Such was the case with a South Asian woman named Mirnha, taken as a slave on a galleon from the Indian Ocean to Manila and across the Pacific, where she became a servant and then a pious Catholic who was declared Caterina de San Juan. Her exotic style reputedly became a template for classic Mexican women's costume, and she represents the studied popularity of the faith convert who becomes herself an object of worship.[2]

Do not miss an opportunity to discuss fashion, which is an engaging way to enter historical thinking. For students with design and style interests, this can be an obvious connection. But it is also a clear and simple way to discuss class, power, prestige, and authority distinctions: consider uniforms, access to ceremonial vestments, or, in the case of island societies, elaborate feather or shell garments and headdresses; also the way that particular textiles — such as the famous pounded-bark tapa cloth of Polynesia — are synonymous with a cultural identity. Later consider how ideas of the clothed and naked, civilized and savage developed and — naturally — for students, what their own wardrobes say about themselves. (Youth? Institutional affiliation? A studied antiformalism? Democratic tendencies? Class status? Self-conscious distinctiveness?)

The galleon trade continued until the nineteenth century and really collapsed definitively as an effective trading system because of revolutions in the Spanish colonies of the Americas. Here Pacific histories, strictly speaking, are inseparable from Latin American histories, and the campaigns of Benito Juárez or Simón Bolívar. More, the Spanish Empire was already uncertain as Manila had been occupied by the British during the Seven Years' War in the 1760s. The British — and French and Americans — would soon challenge the Spanish Lake, as well as the status of the Portuguese, Chinese, Dutch, and Spanish.

The eighteenth century marks a critical juncture in the history of the Pacific, particularly the regions that encompass the islands of Oceania. New language and visions arose from Occidental perspectives, interrogating the existence of noble savages or the devastating effects of European influence upon local cultures. Much of this has to do with the ways that indigenous societies were increasingly impacted by the presence of outlanders from western Europe, succeeding the Iberians and the Netherlanders. By the eighteenth century, the Portuguese were settled in their Asian entrepôts like Goa and Macao. The Spanish were transiting from Manila to the Americas on the galleon routes. The Dutch had built up a commercial and military empire with the Dutch East India Company and were focused on commodities and profit: they had little interest in the Central Pacific, with rich cultures but little in the way of obvious treasures.

The newer seaborne powers, notably the British and French, came with different goals tied materially to changes taking place in Europe itself. Ask the students: Where do they believe their own country or homeland is in a broader historical arc? Civilizations and nations have moments when they are dominant politically, culturally, or economically—and also moments when they decline. Why do some rule at particular times—and then cede that rule to others?

Think of the Enlightenment as a Pacific Category

The framing for this eighteenth-century era is a textbook chapter dedicated to the intellectual and cultural currents of the European Enlightenment. This is always a good place for you to raise the issue of disputed legacies and arguments in history. The outcome is that Pacific islands are rendered through the lens of the state of nature and noble savages, inflecting the more mercantile slave, treasure, and religious conversion narratives of earlier generations. Therefore, do students understand how much it matters when the Oceanian world was explored seriously by Europeans? This particular historical moment defines the Pacific in ways that are different from other parts of the world.[3] This is particularly noted in reports from, for example, Tahiti, where the French explorer Bougainville recorded for posterity his impressions that the local inhabitants were creatures of nature, given over to love and pleasures, and exemplars of a simplicity that had long ago been corrupted in civilized Europe.

Voyagers traveling back (and surviving the trip) to England and France especially were met with royal audiences and taken as curiosities and objects of fashion. In turn, these indigenous travelers, such as the famed Raʻiatean Omai, who ventured to England for two years, were often enthusiastic students of the West, learning what they could. For students, it is always engaging to ask about and debate the meaning of the state of nature. Are humans inherently and naturally good and peaceable? Fundamentally savage, barbaric, and bent on self-preservation? Is the law of nature the necessity of cooperation, or the imperative of killing and survival amid scarce resources? How can any of these perspectives be projected onto other peoples and cultures, and why is this desire to know human nature so profound?[4] Later Islander voyagers in the nineteenth century would come back with knowledge and political and military advantages over rivals. Students should pay attention to and imagine what kind of world Europe might seem to be to an Islander, and what such a voyager might find of interest in such distant lands. This is an excellent teaching opportunity: ask students to defamiliarize themselves with their own everyday surroundings by imagining that they are visitors from another planet, or by reading classic essays like Horace Miner's "Body Ritual among the Nacirema" to see the ordinary in radically unfamiliar ways.[5]

The eighteenth century was a period not only of cultural encounter, but cultural change. An acceleration in applied sciences and knowledge to serve an increasingly technically governed imperial structure led to South Seas missions, the most notable and successful those of James Cook, whose mapping of the Pacific for Western audiences opened entirely new chapters of regional history. It is useful to compare him to other noted English naval predecessors such as Sir Francis Drake, or William Dampier, who were known as much for being privateers and pirates of Spanish shipping as they were navigators. Their fame rested upon armed exploits, and also, in Dampier's case, upon being paired with an Islander named Jeoly, who provided knowledge as a native. This is reminiscent of Magellan and Enrique and their master-slave relationship.

You can also engage students by having them consider the lens from the other end, with discussions about the historical personage of the beachcomber. This figure, generally a solitary Western male sailor, is also associated with the castaway, or the shipwrecked sailor. The noted William Mariner is famed for spending years in the Tongan islands, gradually becoming subject to the life and whims of local island monarchs, providing services and outlander intelligence and skills (and amusement) while being granted, at times, lands, wives, and status among warriors.

Others, sometimes church figures or former missionaries, "go native" and take on the life, manners, and practices (including tattooing and local customs) of their hosts. How do these transitions take place — for Islanders traveling or being kidnapped and taken to Western lands, or Europeans stranded and adapting to new lives at the edge of their known former existence?[6] These are fascinating explorations, as are the noted Western tales that come out of them, such as Daniel Defoe's *Robinson Crusoe*, eternally revived in newer stories of self-reliance and salvation. Challenge the students to imagine and construct their own lives as castaways, survivors, or members of lost communities. Certainly, endless iterations of this theme in popular literature, film, and on television keep the discussions fresh. If stranded, what might the students focus on? What do they think should be prioritized for survival, or while living with local peoples in unfamiliar situations?

Historically, at times, two worlds encountering one another could make common cause. Indeed, it is important to underscore how much was learned from island voyagers like Omai and Ahutoru, who served as sources of information for European navigators, and the ways that discovery and exploration were often the products of knowledge appropriated from locals. The difference in this case is that, where earlier informants were slaves or captives, travelers with Europeans were themselves agents of mobility and knowledge who opened an era that saw laborers, traders, scholars, and adventurers from the islands crisscrossing the ocean on Western vessels. These networks defeated the idea of merely isolated islands. Draw on scholarship by historians like David Chappell, who has chronicled the lives of these remarkable, but often forgotten, individuals. Can students think of other historical figures they've learned about who once were completely unknown, and now have become standard references for history teaching?[7]

Speaking of voyages, you should once again return to Captain James Cook's travels. These are well worth reflection because of what motivated them. The first goal was to find the Great Southern Continent. This legendary land at the bottom of the world was reputed to exist because Western ideas of paradise, mythical kingdoms, and a proper balancing of the globe made it necessary. Careful navigation and record keeping became the hallmark of a particular shift in geographical understanding. As noted earlier, what was demonstrated conclusively was not what was waiting to be discovered, but that things assumed necessarily to be true were not. Cook's last voyage, similarly, was a search for the Northwest Passage around North America from the Atlantic to the Pacific. That, also, existed only in legend — though climate change in recent decades and the melting of Arctic ice has made this more realistic now than in the eighteenth century. Ask students: What other geographical features are legendary, mythical, or enduring in the popular imagination? Think of the lost continent of Atlantis, or El Dorado, the edge of the world where the seas fall off, or King Solomon's Mines, or a score of others.

Pacific history is full of such disputed and contested narratives. The manner in which James Cook was killed in the Hawaiian Islands by local warriors has become a cottage industry of controversy, organized around prominent debates between the anthropologists Marshall Sahlins and Gananath Obeyesekere. Cook first arrived in Hawai'i when the Hawaiians were celebrating a festival of the fertility and growth god Lono. The landing party was treated extravagantly. Was this because there was some sense that the visitors represented the deity? Or was it merely a matter of pragmatic hospitality, custom, and a need to keep powerful strangers on good terms? The central question has long been debated: Do credulous local peoples worship strangers?[8] Students often have many different views on this question.

What is known is that when Cook sailed away from the islands and then unexpectedly returned, he was killed and eaten. Did he come back at the wrong time, or were his own miscalculations of Hawaiian reactions to blame? The controversy can fuel rich debates with students because the world of the Kanaka Maoli — Hawaiian people — is well studied by both indigenous and nonindigenous scholars, who recognize a complex system of both practical and ritual understandings of the world based upon frameworks that have found their ways into Western language: the unifying force and power of life and individual authority, *mana*; the restrictions of the sacred in *tabu* (taboo). Ask students to think of possible ways to try and understand such dense and complex frameworks — can they be analogized to chi, soul, charisma?[9] Many students will be interested in discussing their own understanding of, or longing for, spiritual knowledge, articulation of a life force, or other connection to a nonmaterial world.

Another discussion of engaging interest to students is to consider the meanings of cannibalism. This is a well-worn trope in many histories of encounter, and generally illuminates representational strategies defining civilization and barbarity, enlightened and savage, modern and primitive, or, in the religious framework, the faithful and the heathen. Western observers chronicled the execution of Islander enemies and the consumption of their remains, and more than one explorer (including James Cook himself) was likewise dismembered and eaten. Students can consider the logic around the practice, pursued in either disrespect or great reverence as a way of taking in another's spiritual force through ingestion of another's body, and the outcomes of enhanced status.

For those with a literary bent, a Western classic employing cannibalism precisely as a means to critique the author's own society is Herman Melville's *Typee*, one of his Pacific writings (set in the Marquesas) before the enduring fame of *Moby-Dick*. In the story, a sailor living among the Typee people recognizes their cannibalism yet also comes to appreciate the reasonableness of the act, certainly as he compares it to European religious wars, tortures, dismemberments, and cruelties inflicted by supposedly civilized peoples upon each other across centuries. Ask students to come up with their own examples where the virtues of being civilized seem problematic at best — such as continuing violence, war, or abuse of the environment for the sake of material and economic profit. The questions of the nineteenth century are still those of the twenty-first. To explore broad arguments, like those advanced by scholars such as the cognitive scientist Steven Pinker, consider a perennial debate: Is there real progress in the world, and are things getting better? By what criteria?

The other critical lesson that can be taken from Cook's death, or a more general Pacific-perspective reading of the eighteenth century, is that due to increasing navigational knowledge, chronicles of exploration, and reliable mapping, narratives about the Pacific shifted again. Whereas the Renaissance notion of the Pacific as barbaric and unknown had become the possibly Elysian paradise of natural beings of the Enlightenment, the resurfacing of savagery within portrayals of redeemable (but inferior) Islanders became the creed of large-scale missionary enterprises, along with a dramatic increase in commercial exploitation fostered by new knowledge of whaling, seal hunting, and trade opportunities. These last commercial questions are organized around environmental issues: the harvesting or slaughtering of marine creatures for sale and profit.[10] Do students believe in conservation? Organizations like Greenpeace? Save the Whales?

Thinking about a European and Atlantic historical idea of Enlightenment in a Pacific context can provide original insights into telling not just Pacific but European history. Here you can focus on the eighteenth and early nineteenth centuries, drifting backward and forward across time, making the best use of histories that are about neither colonies nor empires, but zones of interaction and middle grounds, tracing an epoch when shifting authority, tenuous accommodations, and genuine possibilities were the order of the day. In this, rather than presuming eventual colonial despoliation, you can tell histories of peoples, cultures, faiths, states, trading systems, and travelers who came together in significant ways for sustained interaction and commerce over a critical century. It might be easiest to understand the Pacific as increasingly connected by European voyagers and explorers, suggesting the voyaging paths of Dutch, French, Spanish, Portuguese, American, and British explorers and navigators, engaging James Cook, of course, and also names that come up in textbooks and exploration chronicles, such as Quirós, Bering, Wallis, Anson, Tasman, Dampier, Gonzales, Vancouver, and a host of others.

This can provide good methodological opportunities, depending upon the teaching resources at hand. You can, for example, have students study examples of readings from ships' journals, messages, and archival records, and then see how the stories look when contrasted to conventions from European history: the Pacific through the end of the Seven Years' War; the Pacific to the eve of the French Revolution; the Pacific to the beginning of the Napoleonic Empire. Internationalizing the picture is also fairly easy here. Instructors can pay notable attention to the presence of French missions and projects, often driven by strong ideologies of scientific progress, in a sweeping fashion often missed in Anglo-centered historiographies. French names appear, such as Bougainville, but d'Entrecasteaux, La Pérouse, or du Fresne can also be given portraits, along with Pacific Northwest and Russian interests in this period, reincorporating their impact into narratives regularly focused on the South Pacific and the Anglo-American world.[11]

Tie these, then, to settlements and the material bases of commercial connections to the wider world. A discussion of wealth can cover the China trade and familiar markets in furs, sandalwood, and silver, or can survey the same subject in terms of symbolic and status exchanges: the potlatches of the Pacific Northwest, offerings of tapa cloth in Samoa, and the development of curated museum and cabinet of curiosity collectibles — culture made into art — for academies of sciences. These are smart ways for you and the students to think about what otherwise could be just generic categories, by structuring and putting intention behind random lists of objects and commodities. Once again, do students think consciously about what museum collections are?[12] How are they put together? What are they saying about human knowledge?

More, there is also a deeper non-European-focused register to these approaches by emphasizing connected narratives of early Asian, Austronesian, and Polynesian cultures and migrations, spreading widely and settling Asia and Oceania. This can locate the Enlightenment as not just another category of incipient colonial or global transformation. It is a unique moment when, for the first time, the multiple cultures and civilizations that diverged at the end of ancient migrations, which are known today principally through archaeological and linguistic research, once again intersected in a web of continuously interacting communities. The increasing presence of multiple seafaring societies joined through trade and voyaging illustrates convergence, an early version of what would, in another register, be resurrected as globalization. Do students think of this as a form of historical globality?

The alignment of global knowledge in the eighteenth century with science, commerce, and the movement of peoples describes a Pacific not of isolated islands, or a Far East, or distant Southern Ocean or inaccessible

North, but an integrated human world. To get beyond merely representational strategies of encounter, it is once again useful here to adopt the case study or anthropological approach, making good use of key figures or moments to intuit the interests and agencies of many actors. The great coastal chief Maquinna of the Nootka Sound is a good subject for an extended reading for his mastery of political and commercial statecraft, triangulating between his North American Indian people, Chinese merchants, and European fur traders.

All across the Pacific, indigenous identification of plant and animal specimens shaped the categories of early modern taxonomy and the development of natural science. Every teacher will have many students whose interests lie in the biological and life sciences, who can learn about the historical foundations of their disciplines. Thus the intellectual project here wrestles with the aims of natural history and its hope to understand specimens and new plants, animals, and phenomena through classifications and explanatory schemes — the foundation of modern textbooks and teaching.[13]

This, of course, would also be true of classifying humans into races, and trying to understand differences and others, moving toward histories of global commonality, but also vicious hierarchy, condescension, and exploitation though slavery and imperialism. For students, this can be very interesting as a critical disputed legacy in Pacific histories: to consider human ties and their universal expressions, or their particular expressions, by thinking through Islander kinship and exchanges, through *taio* friendship and obligation bonds, sexual relations, and linguistic sharing. All students are interested in the question of what defines friendship, and you can have them elaborate qualities and whether they are common or culturally determined in an always compelling discussion.[14] This means finally not to be rooted in an abstract humanity of the Enlightenment, but in the Enlightenment vision as it developed from oceanic relationships and interactions defined by struggles, conflicts, desires, and negotiations of intimate human ties.

One legacy from the age of European navigational voyages and expanded contacts has been an enduring fixture in European histories: the mutiny on the *Bounty*. This tale of a ship sent from England to Tahiti whose crew mutinied, set adrift its officers, and then disappeared has long crystallized many debated stories of the Pacific. I can recommend referencing this narrative as a teaching device—it is a tale with many filmed and written versions and is a perennial multifaceted lesson for students in many Pacific narratives. The *Bounty* was captained by William Bligh, one of James Cook's former lieutenants, and its journey was to Tahiti, a fabled paradise of indolent reveries and sensual women. The *Bounty* was, moreover, in search of breadfruit plants—an agricultural commodity that the admiralty hoped to grow in the Caribbean to feed plantation slave populations. Thus, the *Bounty* story is really one of global empire, the accommodations and interests of local Tahitian rule, and the attempt to transplant the botanicals of one part of the world to another because of a forced labor population serving colonial planters and imperialism.

The mutiny has been attributed to various causes: both the harshness of the captain and the idyllic lure of the South Seas. Upon being set adrift in a small boat, the castoff Bligh navigated to Dutch territories in the Indies, demonstrating his knowledge of the interconnected Oceanian and Southeast Asian waterways, while the mutineers achieved the legendary dream of pirates, outlaws, and adventurers—they found a tiny uncharted (or at least unfrequented) island, Pitcairn, and established themselves as a new society. Eventually, they killed each other off, though their descendants survived to be rediscovered in the nineteenth century. Students might be surveyed for their knowledge of any number of isolated island scenarios, from classic literature to popular culture—films and television programs—and asked whether those islands are supposed to represent paradise, mystery, or savagery and barbarism. Why does an ideal Western fantasy of leisure involve beaches and palm trees? Historically, at least, what the *Bounty* tale underscores is a story with multiple Tahitian and British actors, one in which an empire with global reach and overlapping commercial, military, and political power was increasingly encroaching upon the Oceanian, Asian, and early modern European Pacific.[15]

Underscore the Importance of Religion

Such conundrums and opportunities in seeking or losing paradise for Islanders, locals, and outlanders were noted in the widespread activity of knowing and learning through spiritual practices. Earlier, we've discussed the cultural and political formations especially around Islam and Buddhism and their roles in shaping learning and rulership in maritime Southeast Asia. Here, you should take advantage of studying some of the Christian evangelical missions throughout the Pacific, notably through two collectives, the American Board and the London Missionary Society. An important approach that derives from this period is the ability to focus on belief as a category; it is one that is wide with possibilities for engaging students in terms of contests and legacies, whether they come from backgrounds of a particular faith or not. The basic narrative is fairly straightforward: Did the Christian word bring salvation, education, and ethical purpose to communities, or was it simply a handmaiden to an ideology of control, cultural erosion, and colonialism? A class can have familiar discussions of missionaries and missions, along with reflections on theology, but also extended thoughts on ideological benefits of improvement and the ways mission groups were interested in animal husbandry, botany, and seed cropping, thus overlapping environmental science thinking with Enlightenment beliefs in Providence and human improvement.

The broader Pacific, strongly Muslim in maritime Southeast Asia and heavily animistic or polytheistic in the Oceanian islands, saw activity by Calvinists, Methodists, Presbyterians, Catholics, and the Church of Latter-day Saints or Mormons. New religious authorities, such as the noted John Williams of the London Missionary Society, were dispatched, but these histories are especially notable for the work of common folk, the famous "godly mechanics" who were expected to preach and teach but also to build, sow, and establish themselves as colonials on foreign soil, or — especially — the "native agents," locally trained preachers who spread the good word as charismatic individuals in their own villages and regions. Ask students how they imagine or have experienced missions and missionaries. It is not uncommon for some students to have been involved in mission work themselves, or to have come from mission-based families or backgrounds. Connections between faith, culture, authority, and history are always interesting to discuss.

Noted Islander preachers like Maretu or Tauʻufa were widely revered and highly influential as they made circuits around Oceania, themselves trained in reading, writing, and speaking, often with powerful results. Many of the trained Polynesian and Islander preachers could develop and, in many ways, lived by the personas and talents of persuasions necessary to attract and keep converts. To disrupt the narrative of Western missionaries attempting to convert local indigenous peoples, it is well worth noting that native agents were quite active in mission work, gaining status and authority for themselves and, in some cases, leaving records of condescension toward non-Christian peoples on other islands. What does this tell us, when the dynamics of faith and power involve not simply Europeans or Westerners and indigenous peoples or natives, but an overlapping series of interests and alliances?[16]

PART II

Devising Strategies

———— *Chapter Five* ————

Imperialism as a Teaching Tool

Recognize the Newer Imperial Powers

If the previous discussions focused on contests around trading partners, Enlightenment framings of flora, fauna, and species, religious and missionary interests, and timeworn tales like those of the *Bounty*, it is important to work with students to see that this period of negotiation and contingency will become more regularized and structured into what historians regard as imperial control, with the increasing power of new seaborne empires. To talk about imperialism requires, of course, at least a general discussion of terms and definitions. Depending upon the instructor, it is helpful to distinguish between periods of mutual exploration and contact, developing interactions, individual or localized ties, and the later-developing impact of statist projects involving commercial, administrative, and military forces, as well as of settler colonialism.

The commanding presence of the British and French — and later, Americans — in the Pacific had antecedents in missionary operations, trade forays, and colonial settlement interests, but they made strong, definitive territorial and political claims for control in the nineteenth century. The models were, initially, somewhat divergent. This does matter, for it is also common with students to immediately jump into Western or European imperialism as the logical outcome of all encounters, with requisite citations of oppression and exploitation. How can you recognize yet complicate this picture?[1] Rather, the focus here is only that empire has a particular place in history and should not be read backward to color a very long period when encounters and engagements were much more tenuous, uncertain, and — one could boldly say — might have led to different outcomes than those that actually developed subsequently.

"Empire" is an unstable term best used with caution when discussing the gradual Western hegemony built upon the encroachment of political, military, and administrative coercive powers in the Pacific Ocean basin in the middle of the nineteenth century. Chronological typing matters. To take the United States as an example, much changed after the Mexican-American War and the land division of the Great Mahele in Hawai'i in the middle of the nineteenth century. It was at this point that definitive models of hegemony on the order of a kind of settler colonialism came to bear. This, and the direct projection of U.S. military naval power toward Japan in the 1850s, clearly mark a sea change.

Discuss Empire through Historical Actors

Broad evocations of empire as an anodyne and relatively meaningless category should be critiqued, and then reconstructed and reexamined through counterexamples of the many agents and actors of the Pacific realms — multiethnic and constantly shifting gangs of sailors, traders, and whalers. One might also include missionaries, migrant laborers, and political functionaries, constituting a maritime labor force. Ask students how they might uncover the stories of such figures, very different from the biographies of great men and women. Where can evidence of these lives be found (rosters, registers, charters, sometimes memoirs)?

A useful teaching approach here is to engage such actors and issues as interwoven narratives. The discussions can be devoted to a large idea (the question of empire) and then elaborated with examples. The focus on individuals as actors is very useful. Too many broad, globally oriented histories are content to frame narratives with categorical types: mariners, Europeans, Islanders, traders, and the like. Underscoring this distinction is important since, after all, understanding motives — even to the individual level where possible — shows where good intentions, calculated self-interest, rank opportunism, protection of family and kin, or outrageous greed and racism all do their work in defining the logic of encounters.

By pulling up a critical focus on specific actors, an instructor can do more than intended by reading against general empire literature: teaching can also resolve to a certain kind of narrative history, one that is figuring out ways to integrate agency and the existential realities of lives into broad categories that otherwise might be dominated by systems approaches. Again, emphasizing this critical approach is important to teaching. Examples are telling. Relate, for example, the dialectic of interest and exploitation between a Hawaiian king like Kamehameha and a sojourning mariner like John Kendrick, which, though not exactly overlapping, forms a keen set of counterpoints — the legendary Hawaiian monarch as read through his mastery of Oceanic statecraft and trade, and the oddly errant American on an endless voyage, the object of which is never quite clear.[2] Such microhistories push against the grain of standard stories of despoiled and declining Polynesians and arrogant, purposeful Westerners rampaging across islands and seas.

Likewise, stories from individual women, such as Mary Brewster's graphic journal of voyaging, interject the presence of male and female gender roles (e.g., domestic civility versus dirty, dangerous whaling experiences) by allowing students to consider their own assumptions about men's and women's labor and the intricacies of everyday life within a broader evocation of Western systems of economic expansion.[3] Can students think of other examples where individuals crossed boundaries, transgressed conventions, or blurred social lines — and with what risks and results?

Of course, "empire" is sometimes wrongly regarded as only a shorthand for Western encroachment upon the Pacific and the world. Brief sketches of Chinese trading masters like Houqua and the merchant monopoly of the Cohong guild in Canton rightly situate the commercial, and sometimes political, power of the Chinese. Such examinations can illuminate the meaning of "empire" partly as an imaginary entity (the China market) and partly as a set of powerful actors with great command of capital. This raises an argument that is a dialectic between scholarly definitions of empire and the individual interests of actors. Teachers can also elaborate around what might be called the corporate bodies of the Pacific to see how constituents of empire might be understood in terms of the sociological organization of whaling, or the institutional, supra-individual structuring of religious orders and practices, the Mandarin ties of the Cohong, or widely disparate, yet equally globally connected scientific missions.[4] What other kinds of groups can students identify in which they align their own identities with institutional allegiances?

Of course, no instructor should deny the coming age of exploitation, and many episodes are already well accounted for in textbooks, such as the Opium Wars and Matthew Perry's missions to open Japan for American expansion into East Asia and the Pacific Islands. Likewise, in narratives of formal arrival, the British established themselves on significant terrain by holding partial control over the island continent of Australia and developing emplacements in New Zealand, as well as primacy in the Fijian islands. The French came somewhat late, having been absorbed in Napoleonic wars and civil strife in Europe for the first half of the nineteenth century, and became strong through military overlordship and gunboat diplomacy as strategies, from Indochina (notably Vietnam) to Tahiti, Moorea, New Caledonia, and parts of Vanuatu, with—for a time—the promise of a French-dominated passage through the Panama Canal.

Perhaps the most notable feature of imperialism in the Pacific is how it obeyed many different models. Do students understand that empires are not monolithic but ever evolving? It is worth suggesting and reviewing that, for example, Australia was a British settler colony growing out of a penal colony in a land diversely populated for some forty thousand years previously by Aboriginal peoples and settlers and traders from Asia. The history is rich and complex and shows how multiple stories can be contained within one national narrative, with the British as one set of actors.

The British landings in what would become Sydney set a grand flag-raising moment of origin for the Australian state as a European settler colony, one linked to and deriving from a legacy of mapping by Cook and other English, French, and Dutch navigators. This story is entwined with the fascinating and harrowing legacy by which the English Australian settlement was conceived, from 1788, as a convict colony—that is, a colonial presence built up by prisoners shipped from England in the hopes of distancing them from the mother country and compelling them to be pioneers in the service of imperial ambitions on the other side of the world. Australian history is full of records, testimonials, court cases, and stunning tales of men and women convicted of what were often petty crimes in a system designed to exploit infractions caused by poverty and desperation, then sentenced and transported to an unknown land.[5] Many of the stories—available in internet databases, archives, and sources—are of death and disease, starvation, hardship, and injustice. Some are of perseverance, struggle, and success in building new lives. Students can reflect upon their own sense of family heritage, of resettling or imagining how to start over in a new land. What are the challenges or promises? What are the stories—hardship, struggle, pride, regret?

These stories are complicated by conflicts on a continent that was not, in fact, as was asserted by English law, empty upon arrival—but widely populated by Aboriginal peoples with ancient and historic cultures occupying a vast array of ecosystems with sophisticated land tenure, resource management, social organization, and spiritual and belief systems, including the famed ability to inhabit a Dreaming realm distinct from material reality. As the English settler colony was premised upon creating farms, towns, and property holders, land appropriation was necessarily built into the logic of colonization—but that land was not empty but occupied, leading to inexorable conflicts, violence, and displacement.

You can have students draw parallels with other histories they may know and reflect on the logic of private property and why that may seem so natural under a particular social and legal regime. More, the idea of indigenous or first peoples, or rightful holders of land and identity, is further complicated in Australia because the English settled in the southeast and only slowly occupied more of the continent. To the north, near Indonesia, trade, intermarriage, and spiritual and ritual exchanges with Makasserese peoples around the Indonesian and New Guinea islands had taken place for generations. Far from a blank slate, Australia as a continent had, in fact, distinctively Aboriginal, Asian, and European communities.[6] The history is less one of discovery and settlement than of how these communities engaged and struggled for accommodation. Students should discuss how often national stories of colonies are about exploration and discovery, when in fact they are about encounter, struggle, and sometimes displacement. What other parallel historical experiences can students relate?

As noted, not all imperial projects followed the initial settler model. Fiji was a partial political concession for protection from increasingly threatening Western powers and internal rivalries. New Zealand was established diplomatically by the Treaty of Waitangi—a negotiated, and disputed, agreement between chiefs and British representatives for shared protection and preserved autonomy, framed by settler depredations, colonial violence, and internecine clan warfare. Regions like Sarawak in Borneo are noted for being taken over by ambitious white colonialists like Rupert Brooke, while the Hawaiian Islands gradually lost indigenous sovereignty because of imported diseases, missionary and planter interests, the legalized breakup of customary landholdings, and the increasing interest of the government of the United States. For the French, the approach was largely gunboat diplomacy: warships and threatened bombardments, landing parties, and forced treaties from Southeast Asia to the Marquesas to the Tahitian Islands and down to New Caledonia.

Episodes and characters can be employed to engage students beyond the categorical discussion of types of empire, from formal to informal, direct and indirect, settler, commercial, and military. Fascinating figures stand out, such as the shrewd warrior Hone Heke, who traveled the world on Western ships from Aotearoa/New Zealand and warred against his rivals, as well as against British occupation of the North Island of New

Zealand, constantly cutting down the flagpoles of the local authorities. The great Fijian chief Cakombau is also a key figure—a wily negotiator, playing off foreign interests and buying and selling influence in the islands, eventually inviting in British protection as a bulwark against the extravagant claims of creditors and colonial settlers.[7]

There is a rich scholarship for studying these periods, and also some engaging pieces of moviemaking, such as Geoff Murphy's noted *Utu*, about the struggle between Maori and Pakeha (white) colonials in late nineteenth-century Aotearoa/New Zealand. This work is particularly notable because the principal character, Te Wheke, is a Maori who works as a scout for the British military, and then launches an anticolonial war against his former allies. Helpfully, there are few obviously heroic or villainous characters—rather, a range of roles from military officers to rebels to clergy to European homesteaders is set against shifting alliances in which few if any come out looking virtuous, and all are trapped within the logic of a colonialism that some recognize and most do not.[8] Can students think of other relevant films or scenarios where the very structures of a society force even well-intentioned characters to turn against each other? This can be a good assignment.

Imperialism is also intriguing to study not only as a system of hegemony or a category of political and commercial exploitation, but as a culture and an experience in which constant negotiations of identity and authority take place. Some students and scholars call this resistance. In some cases, it is really simply the assertion of local indigenous power—a category sometimes overlooked. The Hawaiian Islands are a good case: the great chief Kamehameha unified the islands of the archipelago under his singular rule, earning him the sobriquet "Napoleon of the Pacific," while equally bargaining with, engaging, employing, and holding at bay the Westerners who sought to gain the trade, military force, and influence he controlled at his mid-Pacific crossroads.

This is also certainly true of more modest examples, such as Apolosi Nawai, a villager who saw in an encroaching British presence in Fiji an opportunity to create his own anticolonial and entrepreneurial trading network in bananas, thus challenging and, in a sense, appropriating for local benefit the global connectedness of metropolitan colonials. This is a moment for you to usefully engage students around the question of local economies, small business, or (in modern parlance) entrepreneurship and start-ups, and the role that individual initiative plays in the histories of peoples and cultures around the world. Historians regularly refer to merchants, traders, commerce, and exchange, yet it is useful to think about how small business, from the local shop to the family enterprise or small farm, operates as a bulwark of many regional and national economies, and how it might be similar (profit, service, products) or different (guild or community interdependence) in different contexts. How many students are interested in entrepreneurship, though they may think of it in terms of start-ups? Are they just trying to benefit themselves, or do they see that in some circumstances, such enterprises are challenges to larger powers or monopolies?

Questions of imperialism become particularly interesting to debate when simple colonizer/colonized or victimizer/victimized dichotomies break down. Do give examples and raise questions that explore complexity. In the middle of the nineteenth century, the American Commodore Matthew Perry and his warships famously threatened the Japanese port of Edo with military aggression if trading and concessions were not opened. Japan, in turn, began to launch modern imperial invasions of its own, besting China and seizing overlordship in Taiwan and parts of Korea in the 1890s. Underscoring and demonstrating the ways and degrees of Asian imperialism can be instructive, especially for students who are inured to hearing about Western empires; it is important to maintain a broad understanding of how nations respond to threats, and how they embrace or deflect attributions and adopt self-fashionings as imperial powers themselves. Do students with textbook knowledge see how Japan's rise to world power began not with the twentieth-century Pacific war, but with rival imperial conflicts almost a century earlier?

This gradual and then sudden shifting of power is particularly true for cases like the Hawaiian Islands. American students, for example, are often quite critical of British and French colonial dominance in many parts of the world, yet much more ambiguous about a place like Hawai'i.

Here, versions of bringing progress to locals, or acting to head off inevitable takeovers by other powers, often come to the fore as reasons. Perhaps most interesting is to study the words and works of activist-scholars like Haunani-Kay Trask. Her *From a Native Daughter*, a memoir of trying to be a Hawaiian and an academic philosopher in the context of an uncomprehending establishment at the University of Hawaiʻi, is arresting reading.

Understanding how colonized peoples live in attractive lands but do not benefit socially, politically, culturally, and economically is often challenging. Film here is also particularly valuable. A standard would be *Act of War*, notable not because it is a documentary about Hawaiians, but because it is one of the first comprehensive treatments made by Hawaiians, Kanaka Maoli (people of the land), and represents a critical and activist view of the ways that Hawaiians have struggled to reincorporate their own histories. The defiant statement by Haunani-Kay Trask, "We are not Americans, we will never be Americans," often discomfits students who are perplexed that someone would not wish to be what they value.⁹

Empire was not, of course, simply a political regime, but was intertwined and inextricable from centuries-long commercial interests. Returning to questions of trade and the circles of commerce that crisscross the Pacific is an instructive way to keep together a narrative of the region. To get a fuller picture, we must consider the interconnections between Polynesian commerce, Asian ports, and Melanesian shores. Some of the earliest discussions concerned the silk and spice trades, and now again include whaling, sealing, and silver through the China Trade. Students can think about how huge investments in plantation crops by the nineteenth century begin to dominate world trade—including cotton, but particularly tea, largely from Asia, and sugar from cane plantations across the Polynesian islands. In addition, the particularities of marine products, such as sea cucumber, became more widespread. Each of these items has a particular history and locale: for example, sealing was noted around New Zealand, and particularly toward the Pacific Northwest, and created a thriving and disputed commerce between native North American tribal groups such as the Chinook or Haida, and European and (later) Canadian and American trappers and traders.

For students, it is always useful to recognize that these are not only trade or environmental experiences, but that they continue to be human histories in every sense, particularly for those groups that continue to negotiate the meanings of traditional and modern cultures in contact with global markets. I can recommend the work of Joshua Reid in *The Sea Is My Country*; he has a keen sense for the Makah peoples of the northwest American coast and their "traditional future," which he underscores by framing his study with a 1999 whale hunt that sent pelagic harpooners out in small boats to stalk and return with a humpback. He notes the critical moment that this was in Makah history, much as Polynesian replica canoe voyages and navigation, hunt, and dance revival forms have served as pivots for historical renaissance and strength of heritage assertions throughout Oceania.

Here is where the theme of historical memory, enactment, and reconstruction is so salient. The case provides crosscutting readings of the multiple claims arising from the whale hunt: the animal rights and conservation forces that condemn the practice; the Makah communities that observe customary protocols and await recognition of their heritage; the work of lawyers and judges debating which rights and restrictions apply to the Makah and which to citizens of the United States equally; and, as critically, those who create the records for others beyond the Makah: the media, the commentators, critics. Through it all, the key point is that the act is not a nostalgic yearning for a legendary past, but rather a going forward with the incorporation of an ancient culture.[10] How many traditional practices, rites, or rituals can students identify in their own lives that continue to be valuable in their communities or families even as they embrace the twenty-first century?

Study the Movement of Global Commodities

The experiences of past and present coexisting occur across the worlds of the Pacific. Practices that bring those worlds together—like commerce—are particularly good teaching tools. As an example, trepang, or sea cucumber, is a marine product that was harvested for generations in ways that connected old and new, local and global worlds. The creature was a treasured commodity on tropical islands like the Fijian chain and played a large role in the politics of multilateral trade: local chieftains like Cakombau sold to European traders in exchange for sailing vessels and weapons to conduct local power struggles, and those traders then resold to Chinese markets, enriching themselves and also local trade agents like the Cohong consortiums or Comprador business agents, who managed the finances, contracts, and purchasing of the world in ports like Canton, China.

The globalized world of commerce was very much in evidence already. It is a useful exercise to trace the path of a single product, such as the pelt of a giant sea otter living off the Canadian coastline, beginning with the slaughter of the otter and its pelt as the trophy of a Chinook trapper or hunter; its sale to an American or British agent with commercial ties to China; transshipment across the Hawaiian Islands, perhaps in accordance with demands made by Hawai'i's rulers; display and purchase in Canton as part of a shipment and sale to a merchant and dealer; and, finally, incorporation into an expensive garment.

Ask students to identify products that have made similar peregrinations. For example, the noted study by the economist Petra Rivoli, *The Travels of a T-Shirt in the Global Economy*, describes global economics for a popular audience. Here we can follow the origins of a simple T-shirt, from cotton growing to weaving and sewing in another part of the world, to design and marketing in a wealthy country, to discarded and recycled material in yet another, with strong parallels to textile production in the nineteenth century that connected North America, western Europe, and South Asia.[11] Do students understand basic supply-chain thinking? In addition, many news stories and studies have examined the ways that everything in the current world from automobiles to mobile phones are global in nature and thus hard to track to any one nation or economy. News reports about global competition and trade wars underscore the stakes — and the complications of trying to define a "Made in [particular country]" product.

The cases of fur and food from the Pacific are also environmental histories of marine products and creatures harvested or slaughtered for commercial purposes and profit. Sophisticated histories are built around the ways that these animals and plants made their way from the Americas and Oceania to Asia and the networks of hunters, brokers, agents, and buyers that kept the cycles going for centuries. These stories also tie in with a gradually acquired knowledge of specific species—notably whales, but also seals and botanicals—and the ways that their mobility, by both migration and transport (or in the case of plants, recultivating), has radically shaped the modern world by leading to the growth of entire industries (like whaling), the decimation or outright extinction of species (other marine mammals like Steller's sea cow), or the growth of monopolies and plantation economies (from spices to sugar and cotton). Through these histories of trade and transfer, the key points of environmental and ecological narratives are underscored, not categorically, but through relating very material examples of human interactions with the nonhuman world. The lore and practice of whaling, sealing, and harvesting of marine creatures has been studied by historian Ryan Jones and many others.[12]

Some of the classic studies of the environmental historian Alfred Crosby's ecological imperialism and the impact of introduced germs, diseases, and plant and animal species into new environments also fall in this domain. This area will particularly interest students focused on medicine or public health. How did traders, agents, rulers, and eventually colonial authorities think about the connections between disease and transfer of goods? Records show that indigenous populations were severely impacted by contagious diseases carried by Europeans, and that this issue continued into the twentieth century. The influenza epidemic of 1918, which killed significant populations in the Pacific Islands, was transmitted along with the cargoes and crews of visiting ships. Where public health policy failed to protect local peoples is a worthy study of its own.

Officials often blamed locals for the nature of their villages, the hygiene of their homes or eating practices, or the supposed ignorance of mothers who failed to keep their children healthy. Almost never directly cited was the role of those officials in introducing contagions through their trade and settlement policies. Students can certainly relate this to issues in their own lives. They may think of different strains of the flu, hepatitis, or Zika virus or Ebola. Who deserves to be protected? When should individuals or communities be quarantined? Should parents have the choice not to vaccinate their children, or is a larger public health issue at stake?

On a related note, do you think your students will be interested in the history of excrement? You can tie other commodity histories to Gregory Cushman's detailed and fascinating recounting of the history of guano, the nitrogen-rich fertilizer of bird droppings, harvested from islands off the coast of South America, which pulls together narratives of avian nesting, oceanic and insular biomes, forced human labor, global competition, regional warfare, and legal and territorial claims to control a highly valuable natural substance in an era—the nineteenth century—before the widespread employment of industrial and chemical fertilizers.[13]

In fact, many exercises can be developed around what, academically, might be thought of as natural resource extraction, commodity chains, and—in business—supply chain management. Popular and scholarly works dedicated to single commodities are good examples of this approach: consider the above-mentioned work on guano, or any number of books on the Hawaiian pineapple or the production and distribution of tea. These discussions are easily materialized with a box of tea, a sachet, or a piece of fruit. Where does it come from? How did it get where it is? What labor and which people were involved in delivering it to where the students are, today? A teacher can focus on luxury trades like fur in the nineteenth century, which, though very lucrative, were still dwarfed by the enormous revenues from cash crops like tea and opium. The linkage is well known: running a dangerous and possibly bankrupting trade balance to pay for tea addiction, British merchants sought products to sell back to China and developed a captive opium market, drawing on production from their crown colony in India. Attempts to limit this trade by Chinese officials like Lin Zexu led to open conflict in the notorious Opium Wars of the 1840s, in which British gunboats and landing parties forced open Chinese markets to ensure that the profitable trade would continue.[14]

If opium seems too esoteric to grasp as a visceral teaching tool, students can be asked to think about other addictive opiates and the economic, political, and social distortions they cause: the global movements of, for example, heroin and cocaine, and more recent chemical derivatives. Students can think about the abuse of prescription medicines and painkillers, and debates about public health crises like opioid abuse. How do these issues impact both individuals and communities? How do profit and criminality arise in tandem in ways not necessarily the same in other businesses? Who protects these interests, and why are the challenges so difficult?

More broadly and historiographically, students can reflect on the ways that wars and battles over commodities ripple throughout history, whether for control of sugar and cotton plantations or oil and gas. Wars for fossil fuels are familiar in twentieth-century history. Students can also study questions about commodity chains more broadly and the degree to which the gradual global dominance of the West beginning in the early modern period was increasingly predicated upon providing chemical stimulants to enable physical labor for industrial work: sugar, tobacco, opium, caffeine-containing coffee and tea, all of them (like spices) at one time cultivated with forced labor, often in plantation systems, under regimes of imperial political and economic control. Discuss with students how many of them could not get through a day without sugar and caffeine in some form; how many smoke; how many are — in a sense — chemically dependent on former plantation crops in order to be productive in their work.[15]

Ocean-specific sources of marine wealth and trade were numerous. They ranged from sea cucumbers to the skins of otters and seals, to sugarcane from plantations, copra from coconuts, and oil from whales, all requiring highly structured and specialized regimes of labor. The skills of farmers, fishermen, and tidal scavengers were organized to serve villages and local communities. Ask your students to think globally. Why do local economies shift? Students can try to find parallels in ways that distant demand can compel massive change locally. How do bad winters, scorching summers, or political upheaval in one part of the world come to impact the price of wheat, produce, or commodities like heating oil and gold in other parts of the globe? How does the cultivation of corn for ethanol fuel production in one country affect the price of corn flour and tortillas in another?

Focus on the Everyday Life of Labor

Logically, then, the tracing of trade and commerce in the nineteenth century is only partly a story of commodities, circuits, and transfers of wealth. It is, inescapably, largely a narrative about labor — especially, about a single question: Whose labor? Definitely do challenge students to think through the ways that different skills were tied to the growing of crops or living organisms, the creation of valuable products from those crops, and how those became worldwide commodities. Interestingly, labor itself provides a way to talk about networks of connection that defined imperial reach, in ways readily accessible to undergraduate students. As the historian Frances Steel points out, colonial interests in New Zealand, Australia, and Fiji were almost inconceivable without steamship lines: liners, tramps, merchant regulations, and debates about shipping legislation were parts of a grand imperial question. But who really built and worked the empire? Steel's approach is to focus on a single provider out of New Zealand, the Union Steam Ship Company, and to chart the local configurations of regional trade and transportation networks.[16] Such an approach gives you, the instructor, the opportunity to think about and search out lives — crews and servants, the ready and often anonymous hands from multiple Islander and Asian cultures, the wharf laborers and steerage passengers who left their traces in the historical records. In this, Pacific history can recognize the lives of unknown yet critical actors within the grand narratives of interregional relations in the Pacific.

How to do this? One way to get at the materiality of such histories — absent actors to uncover or interview — is at least to reconstruct the environments in which such actors labored. Students can do excellent research through collections of nautical artifacts and museums, pictures of docksides, and studies of engines and technological culture. Points of focus are not only the ingenuity of ship design, but evolving meanings, particularly in the opulent passenger liner, a phantasmagoria of a class society built upon commercial wealth, a floating hotel replete with smoking rooms, plush upholstery, antique furniture, and impeccable service by servants. What environments do students know that convey class, whether hotels, restaurants, or entertainment halls?

Such studies also indicate the presumed roles of laborers, servants, and different classes of passengers, as well as proper roles for males and females, here where the domestic sphere of home and comfort is transposed into the traditional realm of sailors and seafaring men. In turn, students can ponder how ascriptions of femininity were transferred to male Indian and Asian servants as shipboard work became rapidly deskilled in the age of steam. The age of "old salts" was passing. Skilled sailors with mastery of rigging gave way to ships run by managers with technical certification, leaving crewmen little more than manual labor to do. Ask students, what kind of jobs change in meaning as the ratio of men to women performing them also changes over time? What has happened in teaching? Nursing and health care? Which sectors have remained the same?

Importantly, this leads to examining the necessary connections between multiracial maritime labor and land-based labor policies shaped by colonial anti-immigrant racism. Do you want to have a discussion of Pacific anti-immigrant policies? Discuss past and present arguments — in the early twentieth century in Australasia these were tied to fears of Chinese labor, leading to promotion of a nativist politics: worthy, virtuous, but cheated Europeans being denied work and pushed out of employment by an influx of cheap, cowardly Asians, who presumably brought crime and disorder. It should be easy for students and teachers in multiple contexts to see how these arguments about immigration, securing borders, free labor and opportunity, or cheap labor and taking away jobs become highly politicized. Political leaders often exploit the fear that immigrants will be dangerous, will not fit into established national cultures, and will ruin those cultures. Is exclusion an answer?[17]

The laboring voices themselves are, as often, muted in the records, so critical approaches are necessary to excavate them. The most fruitful strategy is to focus on patterns of action rather than words, and to note strikes, protests, or group actions to challenge inequities, prejudice, discrimination, and violence. Students should be encouraged to study social histories of the experience of laborers as people, not just statistics.[18] Many students can relate these stories to other familiar narratives of immigration, migration, displacement, even refugee status, with all of their attendant complications.

With the advent of global markets and large-scale capitalization of acreage and farming plots, labor forces numbering in the hundreds were required by managers and planters, leading to plantation systems across island chains, notably from Fiji — where Indian contract labor was brought in from South Asia — to the Hawaiian Islands, where cane workers formed a polyglot society of largely Japanese, Chinese, Filipino, Hawaiian, and Portuguese workers under tiers of overseers called *lunas*. It is extremely helpful for students to tack back and forth between large questions of systems by locating those labor regimes within narrations of everyday life — the social and material experience of individuals and communities on the ground. These experiences are often captured in first-person tales, or in dioramas or museum reconstructions. What was life like? What were the foods? The dress, songs, daily rituals? The nature of work, friendship, and education? Teachers can draw from innumerable examples of these narrations from the daily life of laborers.

Likewise for other work regimes: discuss with students the ways that different organizational units — the plantation, the wharf and dock, the sailing ship — are all labor organizations, often multinational. The world of whaling, harsh and dangerous, took crews of Kanaka islanders, Asians, lascars, and other crew members drawn from ports around the world under Euro-American captains on long voyages chasing sperm whales and seals for blubber and oil. Rulers like the Fijian chieftain Cakombau required his own people to scour reefs and tidal flats for sea cucumber, and islanders from the Solomons were not only bound by harsh contracts, but also at times treated as near-slaves under forced contract labor — a practice known as "blackbirding" — to serve on cotton and pineapple plantations in northern Australia or in Fiji. For students in the United States, it is interesting to note that such plantations in the Pacific world became briefly profitable because of the American Civil War — which led to the blockade of Southern cotton exports and increasing demand from mills in England, for example, for alternative sources.[19]

Critically, as previously noted, the struggles of everyday life are a key part of understanding labor. This is a part of the course where students from many different traditions can surely contribute some tales and oral histories — perhaps from grandparents or parents, in stories of immigration, resettlement in a new country, and the establishment of an identity, work, and family. In fact, students should be asked to consciously reflect on the meaning of immigrant experience not only as a historic study but as a continuing, living phenomenon, parsing out familiar questions: What are the immediately notable differences between the former life and the new? What expectations and realities have been met? How have newcomers been treated? What are the reactions of new acquaintances, as well as of family who remain in the former country? Historians like Ron Takaki, Gary Okihiro, Evelyn Hu-Dehart, and Mae Ngai have woven together testimonials and personal stories of living conditions, food, politics, and everyday triumphs and failures. The stories of exploitation, mistreatment, and at times murder of captives are stunning, though so are the tales of survival, resilience, and rebuilding of lives in new homelands, as in the Indian community in Fiji, also widely and personally chronicled by scholars like Brij Lal.[20] Moreover, though such narratives regularly focus on struggle, prejudice, overcoming, and difficulties, success stories are also part of their scope. What stories come from students' own families about migration, searches for opportunity, community building, or alienation?

You should not forget to discuss the personal success of particular figures, even while underscoring the relentless struggle of most laboring communities. Some unique individuals, like the Islander Kwaisulia, benefited from commerce by using his talents, first as a simple contract laborer, to himself become a coastal chief, brokering deals for workers with local villagers, adventurers, and recruiters offering goods and commissions. Tales of hope, suffering, dislocation, abuse, ambition, and achievement are all true, woven into historical narratives. In what cases and why do some figures achieve this success, while so many others do not? How are these stories then used by others as proof of hard work, opportunity, or unfairness? Why do stereotypes around "eternal aliens," or "model minorities" arise, and who is behind them? These are excellent teaching questions.

Keep Geography in Mind

Mobility of workers and transformation of labor migration networks forged new flows and links between Asia, Australia, and the Americas. Rather than the better-known scholarship on the United States or Hawai'i, you could focus on the Pacific coast of South America, for example, Chile. It is important to remember — and often overlooked — that Mexico, South America, and Canada have had critical roles in Pacific histories, as has been noted by the anthropologists Eveline Durr and Philipp Schorch.[21] So much of contemporary Pacific discourse is framed by the United States and China (the U.S. especially looms large in Pacific Rim formulations). It is important, however, not to equate China with East Asia — a generation ago all focus was on the Asian Tigers in general, and before that Japan, not to mention the entire record of early modern exchanges and interaction. Once again, historicizing the Pacific is a matter of discovering boundaries and connections, not presuming them from geography.

A vision of a truly transpacific Pacific must shine through a new geography and examples, and through networks of indigenous actors who populate mobile, connected, and often mutually supportive quests, claims, and causes. This can work especially if teachers find sensible ways to rethink the Pacific historiographically: as a crosscutting series of linkages between the Americas and the North and South Pacific. At first glance, this might not seem particularly new, but one can avoid the Pacific Rim trap — of simply thinking of North America as the United States and of East Asia as Japan and China — by redefining a more widely generous (and overdue) geography for the Americas, plural, by engaging Canada, Mexico, and South America, especially the Pacific-facing regions from Central America to Peru, Ecuador, and Chile. Much new historical work has studied Chinese migrations to New Spain/Mexico and to South America, or Japanese communities in Peru and Brazil.

Hawai'i, though (disputedly) part of the United States, can be examined in terms of Mexican community presence and transoceanic connections, rather than the important but more familiar Asian, haole (white), and Kanaka Maoli interactions. This involves understanding how conventional wisdom — that Hawai'i is very much an Oceanian and Asian state — actually serves effectively to make Hispanic immigrants, especially Mexican in this case, almost invisible. This is fascinating. Mexican migration into the continental United States is regularly part of a huge hemispheric political debate, yet Hawai'i is somehow not part of this debate, or is held as a case apart. Why is this? Why do students think some kinds of immigration get a lot of attention, while others are ignored?

In this way, the black-white-Latino triangle of race relations can be rethought by looking at U.S. imperialism generally, and different coalitions, integrations, and conflicts between Asians, Mexicans, and descendants of the Hawaiian kingdom overall. David Chang, himself an indigenous Hawaiian scholar, has provided excellent insight into the enormous transoceanic and intercultural vision of the Hawaiian people before contact with Westerners and since, in *The World and All the Things upon It*. Chang particularly points out how Hawaiian cosmologies and literary stories illustrate the connectedness of Oceanian peoples to all parts of the globe, and how Kanaka Maoli/Hawaiian communities became trading partners, laborers, friends, and the husbands and wives of non–Pacific Islander peoples, including whites (haoles) but also Native Americans and African Americans.[22] His work underscores the ways in which too many histories are about Westerners as white Europeans and their engagements with island peoples, rather than the much more complex relationships between peoples of multiple cultures, histories, and origins.

Equally, newer scholarship can regularly contradict assumptions about historical actors, with comparisons and alignments that seem evident and logical but which are not highly visible in mainstream scholarship: comparisons between Barbados and Fiji; regional imaginings connecting Australia and Chile; human remains repatriation in Mexico and Australia; transpositions between New Zealand and Canada, Hawai'i and Mexico. This is original scholarship in the best sense. It may also not be where you wish to begin. You may find such work to be challenging and perhaps complicated to address in the course of teaching a general survey. However, specific assignments, and certainly student projects, can be organized around thinking through Pacific histories as intersecting with new narratives that break apart conventional narratives. Encourage students to search or even posit juxtapositions that will create new ways of thinking about historical materials. This is very much an assemblage model.

Some examples perpetually fascinate. Every year that I have taught Pacific and Oceanian histories, there are always students who want to learn more about Rapa Nui/Easter Island. Whether this is part of a fascination with unsolved mysteries, or an acquaintance with, say, the theories of Jared Diamond about civilizational collapse, most of the focus is on the famous moai (stone heads) and the history of slavery. Imagining Easter Island in terms of indigenous music and dance forms is less familiar. This approach is therefore salutary, and can be employed in multiple contexts. Performed culture studies of Hawai'i, Tahiti, and other Polynesian states are sophisticated, and combining the two allows a view of what is often missed in assessing Chilean rule over Easter Island — a complicated and mixed series of indigenous and Chilean nationalisms in tension over cultural identity. Students then may see that the simple island mystery narrative becomes a historical study of the connections between Pacific Islanders, Latin American histories, and global culture.

It is always useful to encourage students to investigate the ways that Pacific peoples are political actors, a point often missed because of touristic representations of happy, smiling locals, and to look into the pan-Pacific and global indigenous international of shared interests, often anticolonial. The network of indigenous actors is a great theme and relates to other circuits of actors from other parts of the world. Students are often interested in understanding something of their own experience by studying how institutions of education and learning operate in global contexts. Any number of projects can be developed by looking into school systems, curricula, textbooks, and the language of pedagogy from Canada to Mexico and southward across the Pacific Basin.

Focusing on such dialectics between national identities and smaller communities has enormously rich possibilities in terms of understanding local experiences of larger political, economic, and cultural forces. An example would be the Pacific Northwest as an often-neglected territory of study, at least until recently. Interesting work has been done, for example, that now concentrates on Filipino and Chilean exiles in the region. Urban locales like the port city of Seattle, though obviously in the U.S., can be resituated as a framework for the claims of Chilean and Filipino activists, rather than tales of immigration and assimilation. Here, Chilean immigrants are connected to the Pacific through a continental displacement, from south to north, shaped through a community distant from their putative home. The same applies to Filipinos in adjacent neighborhoods, now living different lives after migrating from the Philippines after protesting against the Ferdinand Marcos regime.[23]

You can encourage students to understand and engage with families of Vietnamese and Cambodian origins likewise. These are often studies of dislocation, yet they are not fundamentally stories of Americanization or identity but rather of alliance and fracture in looking toward a broader, global anti-imperialist set of struggles. What communities have particular presence or impact in your own region or locality? How do different communities interact where you live? Is there a dominant culture, or not?

——— *Chapter Six* ———

Anthropology and Ethnology as Teaching Tools

Understand the Role of Anthropology

Pacific histories—those that connect the Oceanian islands with Asia and the Americas—are particularly notable because of the ways they have developed institutionally. Contentious historiographical arguments course through the field, which was not established along the lines of, say, the legacy of a Western tradition tracing to Herodotus, or Shang oracle bones that are inscribed artifacts and written records in ancient China, or even the ideagraphic and representational transmissions of the great civilizations of Mesoamerica. This is not to say that the Pacific was not studied, but that the scholarly work issued largely from anthropology, ethnology, linguistics, archaeology, and fields often dedicated initially to ancient societies sometimes called primitive, often deemed highly ritualistic and temporally static. Ask students their impressions of peoples that they think to be unchanged, or of places that time forgot.

Anthropology as both a subject and methodology is particularly rich with insights. For one, it has been the discipline that first reinforced, and later troubled, the boundaries between the primitive and the modern, and helped shift discussions of peoples globally away from civilizations (presumed to pertain largely to Western societies) and toward cultures, a recognition of the diversity and value of multiple practices and systems of social, political, and economic organization. The history of the discipline is notable for its impact in terms of thinking about comparative cultures. What do students think about anthropology? Will most of them recall researchers with notebooks, living in villages, or making documentary films in jungle settings? Whereas earlier studies were the work of intellectuals, assembling interpretive frameworks out of evidence delivered by voyagers, missionaries, traders, and colonial agents, the twentieth century did see the advent of a practice based upon fieldwork, and the beginning of participant observation.

Ultimately, the question becomes, Who is studying whom? In classic histories of anthropology as a discipline, Bronislaw Malinowski is most famous, particularly for his work in the Trobriand Islands, simultaneously astounding the world with his studies of ritual, sexuality, and symbolic exchange in trade—the famed Kula rings of gifts and spiritual power in the island chains—while also working within the framework of British colonial supply lines and administrative authority. The estimable Margaret Mead wrote her best-selling *Coming of Age in Samoa* to reveal the uninhibited attitudes of young Samoan women about love and intimacy, at once critiquing Western morals yet also reinforcing the idea that Islanders are simple, timeless, and natural beings, untouched by historical changes.[1]

Here is an always engaging opportunity for students to consider how other cultures are typically represented, particularly in popular culture, and especially in terms of the signs and symbols of the primitive compared to the modern. What are the presumed satisfactions and discontents of each? Why are highly urbanized citizens of industrial cultures often susceptible to touristic images of empty islands and beaches? Why do indigenous peoples inhabiting these landscapes often want more technology, more infrastructure, and greater access to material goods? Examples can be drawn especially from the ways that Oceanian cultures have been widely represented: through museum collections. You can return to approaching your lessons through artifacts, as proposed in the first chapter, or introduce material culture objects at an appropriate point, trying to reconstruct the lifeways that produced them. Museum collections tend to place objects in protective cases, thus preserving yet abstracting them from living contexts, which allows clarity about the actual artifact yet imbues it with an ahistorical stasis as a fixed moment of representation. Ask how museums tend to freeze histories, and how such institutions in turn try to bring contexts back to life through reconstructions, dioramas, virtual technology displays, or testimonies from living communities.

Likewise, students can be engaged with drawings and engravings in historical sources, and photographs and images taken in ethnographic fieldwork. Many tend to record ceremonies, dances, and rituals—which are dramatic, colorful, and representative of special occasions, not daily materiality. Some, dated from the late nineteenth and early twentieth centuries, were, in fact, staged in studios, where elements such as artificial palm trees or a tropical backdrop reflect a Western imagining of Pacific life. What is left out or included in such images? Why do many pictures seem so inherently folkoric, and lacking in the work and challenges of everyday life? You might even ask students about social media on the internet, and how it encourages an idealized presentation of one's own life and circumstances in order to impress others.

Connect Nationalist Identities

The question of authenticity—that is, overcoming an idealized indigenous existence—was a key element for early antisettler and anticolonial struggles in the nineteenth century, especially as they began to evolve into genuinely nationalist movements by the early twentieth. That is to say, indigenous peoples and local communities also studied and learned from their putative masters about political organization and cultural and economic assertiveness. Have students compare the postcard representation of local peoples—folkloric, colorful, costumed, often smiling—with the political and nationalist struggles taking place around Asia and Oceania.

CHAPTER SIX

The logic of these struggles was rooted in local clashes and discontent under colonial rule, but they did not spring up simply through ideological self-awareness.

Ideas and activism spread along commercial and trading routes, and colonial administrations' use of subject workers and bureaucrats supported a structure of privileged yet prejudicially excluded functionaries from positions of real authority. Literacy and communication networks abetted the process, as did key figures such as, in the Indonesian islands, the writer and soon-to-be national heroine Kartini, who wrote eloquently about her lack of opportunities as a woman in a world dominated by men and tradition.[2] Students can certainly debate the degrees to which the very institutions, technologies, and training needed to support imperial systems also inherently provide spaces for critique and resistance, as well as the foundations for flowering local and national identities. How does education, for example, in a dominant language, culture, or set of principles also create the potential for a colonial subject to use those tools against existing authorities? In Kartini's case, why do entire areas of work or profession still seem largely dominated by men? Which ones, and why?

The widespread flowering of questioning in the name of change was truly empowered by the recognition of global transformations and political agitation around the world. From the late nineteenth century, a rapidly industrializing Japan had organized to overcome the terms imposed by Matthew Perry's black ships in Edo Bay, and then became itself an imperialist force, battling against both China and Russia in the Sino-Japanese (1894–95) and Russo-Japanese wars (1904–5), besting both great empires in military conflicts and controlling territorial spheres of influence in Taiwan, Korea, and the Sakhalin peninsula.

Teachers and former contract laborers like Totaram Sanadhya in Fiji were meeting independence activists in South Asia, and Manilal Maganlal Doctor, a lawyer, traveled on a circuit that rivaled that of Mohandas Gandhi, speaking before the Indian National Congress and connecting London, South Africa, the Indian Ocean, and a worldwide band of organizers through his work in the Fijian islands. This is an important point for teaching Pacific histories: these were not isolated societies or polities.[3] While most populations rarely left their local areas or were tied by labor or obligation to their lands, key figures were highly mobile and circulated not only through the Pacific but around the world.

Ideas and writings also moved quickly. Political insurgencies called for change in the Indonesian islands, as groups like the Budi Utomo and Sarekat Islam formed cooperatives, and political representation congresses allied against the rule of Dutch administrators. Understanding nationalism partly as the expression of a people with an imagined community, in Benedict Anderson's formulation, is worthwhile for students to explore — not only in assertions of patriotism but as a powerful organizing principle for those seeing nations as goals and promises of a united people and community.

Students should certainly be encouraged to consider what nationalism means to them. What are its elements, and which identities and definitions are contested, whether as Americans, Fijians, Indonesians, Filipinos, Australians, Mexicans, British, Chinese, Koreans, or the like? Are students patriotic? Are they proud of their own country or way of life? Which elements do they consider to be the most critical — loyalty to institutions and leaders? Adherence to common principles? Traditions of struggle and overcoming, including the immigrant narrative? A simple teaching narrative could describe the colonial period in the Pacific as dominated by hegemonic, military-controlled, imperially administered settler colonies with subject populations, gradually contested and troubled by nationalist movements and internal contradictions. This is, of course, overly simplistic, but not entirely without value. Students should be encouraged to learn more about particular instances and locations of formal, anticolonial movements and violence, such as occurred in Samoa during the resistance called the Mau, or the Chinese national self-assertion led by Dr. Sun Yat-sen.[4]

Some demands for national sovereignty went far beyond autonomy and self-determination and instead became challenges to the global imperial order. Students will already have ideas about revolutions, such as the American Revolution in what became the United States, the French Revolution, the Haitian Revolution, the Chinese Revolution, the Russian Revolution, or the Iranian Revolution. Do students have knowledge about or received views on revolutions? Can they give examples of progress and liberation? Or extremism and chaos? Why, where, and in which cases do we make these judgments?

—— *Chapter Seven* ——

Conflict as a Teaching Tool

How Does War Shape History?

In the Pacific, nationalist and imperialist strategic struggles broke out into violence, armed conflict, and, by the middle twentieth century, large-scale mechanized slaughter. This manifested particularly in the collision of empires: in Asia, notably between the Japanese and Chinese, and then with the United States and European colonial powers, shaped by the parallel rise of fascism in Italy and Nazism in Germany, and the collapse of imagined collective security during World War II.

In the mid-twentieth century, the Pacific was a major theater of global conflict, and Islander peoples were drawn into warfare, alliances, and loyalties with the coming of the Japanese, Americans, and Europeans. They were involved in co-operation and resistance, military volunteerism and conscription. In particular, it is useful for students to examine figures and communities generally overlooked when teaching the Pacific War as a conflict between Japanese and Allied forces. To understand the role of Fijian and Samoan fighting forces in campaigns in Oceania—and also in Europe, as part of imperial armies requisitioned from around the world—students might trace the career of a heroic individual like Jacob Vouza, a scout and intelligence operative who passed secrets back and forth across military lines, partly by feigning an ignorance of the larger conflicts and performing the role of the simple islander.[1] Students can discuss the ways that some groups and individuals achieve their aims by pretending to be the thing that others imagine them to be (in this case, a native).

It is important to teach that Islanders were not merely victims or bystanders to conflict, but active players negotiating their own survival or advantage. Across frontiers, communities raised provisions and funds for war materiel and supplies, and many were trapped in dangerous situations—pushed or shuffled back and forth in their own homelands between occupying military forces, bombed by one, supporting another, changing alliances pragmatically, trying to avoid starvation, violence, and execution. How can appearing to be a noncombatant—and especially a primitive or savage—be an advantage to local peoples? Is it ever possible to be "neutral," and in what cases?

Students may be familiar with many events in world history across the wider Asia-Pacific, such as the Japanese invasion of Manchuria and the atrocities of the Rape of Nanjing; the collapse of British Singapore, the retreat of American military forces in the Philippines, and the Bataan Death March; or the jungle war of Australian, British, and New Zealand troops in Papua New Guinea, supported by Melanesian islander guides, scouts, porters, nurses, and operatives denominated the "fuzzy wuzzy angels." A focus on these supposedly minor players in the war—that is, not the generals, and far from the strategy making of military leaders—highlights the lived experience of warfare.[2] If your school has access to oral history archives or first-person accounts of veterans, they can become invaluable sources in constructing an on-the-ground understanding.

The American war is historically marked by the Japanese bombing of Pearl Harbor in December 1941, and a series of battles that are epochal in military history: the aircraft carrier battle of Midway, the island-hopping strategy of controlling territories, the land and sea wars around the

Solomon Islands (including the rescue of future U.S. president John F. Kennedy, abetted by Islanders), the famed and bloody battle for Guadalcanal, and the war for and raising of the flag on the island of Iwo Jima. I often show historic images from these conflicts as part of a journey into military history, and am always impressed at how many students are steeped in war history and can identify key battles and moments. What other images come to mind for students? Which key military events figure in the teaching and museum displays of different countries?

World War II, as most students know, reached a diplomatic and military conclusion with the complex and highly debated legacies of the dropping of atomic bombs on Hiroshima and Nagasaki. This is a singular historical moment that resonates across generations in many ways. Students should learn about debates over textbook revision in Japan, the role of the military in society, the self-vicitimization of the Japanese as a result of bombings, and the renunciation-of-war constitution written and promulgated during the American occupation under General Douglas MacArthur.

In the United States, continued arguments about the necessity of atomic warfare, and fear of the USSR with the encroaching Cold War, shaped subsequent histories that greatly marked the Pacific. All of these are staples for historical debate with students: Is atomic warfare ever justified? Did it save lives or was it racist in nature? How do questions of war guilt and responsibility weigh on the Pacific?[3] Broader legacies of the war and oral histories of former combatants and participants are typically of great interest to students. Almost every class includes students whose grandparents or other relatives had experiences of the Pacific War, or have transmitted stories and legacies from family members and friends of another generation.

Understand the Importance of Decolonization

One of the outcomes of the Pacific War was a weakening of the European colonial powers. In Asia, memories of the postwar period work differently depending upon the location and identity of conquering and subject populations. The fragmentation of former colonial empires, including Indochina, led to Vietnamese insurgency against the French, China under Mao

Zedong ousting Chiang Kai-shek, Korea being divided into North and South, Indonesia undergoing a nationalist revolution against Dutch rule, and the Philippines evolving toward independence under American colonial authority. In Oceania, islands became trust territories, mandates, and strategic bases in the Cold War, leading to a reorganized political map of the Pacific. The effects of Soviet-American tensions looped back to frame global conflicts through crises in China, Taiwan, Korea, and Vietnam.[4]

Notably, these struggles were strategic maneuvers not only in the context of a political and ideological Cold War theater. They were intensely localized, and in these cases the battles were less about titanic issues of communism versus capitalism than matters of local autonomy and authority, framed around decolonization and development. Ask students to reflect on the ways that big ideological and military histories often look like personal and community quests for independence at a local level. Grand strategy by political leaders in national capitals is experienced close to home in the form of rallies, meetings — or street protests. In the later twentieth century, a generation defined itself as children of the Cold War. In the twenty-first century, how do students understand the key markers, and personal commitments, that define their own generation in terms of globe-spanning tensions and conflicts? What are their issues?

The Pacific islands experienced national liberation struggles, and these became the foundations of how the history of the Pacific region is told. It is worth noting for students that the first chair in Pacific history was not established until the 1950s in Australia and, perhaps more to the point, that Oceanian history was previously regarded as a subset of imperial or colonial history. Thus, much of what would be considered documented historical record and narrative was produced in terms of decisions made in London, Canberra, Paris, or Washington, DC, and local peoples and cultures were acted upon as subjects.

This changed in the postwar period, consonant not particularly with any new historical consciousness but with the impacts of decolonization movements around the world that challenged and ultimately transformed many formerly colonial concessions. Make sure to teach these parts of the history of the Pacific in the context of global history. Understand that what was happening in Oceania was part of a general phenomenon that included the Middle East and sub-Saharan Africa, and was underscored globally in conflicts that ranged from Indian independence under the leadership of Mohandas Gandhi to the establishment of the People's Republic of China under Mao Zedong, ousting Chiang Kai-shek's Nationalist forces to Taiwan; and the legacies of Ho Chi Minh and the creation of a communist-controlled North Vietnam, which became a united Vietnam with the collapse of French and then American forces between the 1950s and 1970s.[5] Studies of Chinese, French, and American history will lead to comparing and contrasting the Vietnam experience less in terms of the hubris and faulty policy of military and political leaders than of the experience of veterans of the war from all sides, as recounted in memoirs and, increasingly, museums and commemorative events. Are students familiar with these sources, including oral histories, monuments, and memoirs?

Throughout the Pacific, both Asia and Oceania, changes were taking place. Perhaps the most salient way to teach these transformations is through framing regions as nodes of a global network where activists, agitators, political figures, and others traveled to shape new consciousness and programs for change. The scholar Tracey Banivanua-Mar has done excellent work in outlining the principal engagements: the ways that Asian and Islander peoples demanded rights and recognition in global forums, including the early twentieth-century decisions in Versailles that set the diplomatic and political template for the post–World War I era.[6] While teaching, don't forget to emphasize broader trends such as the rise of networks of communicators, including radio broadcasters, writers, and journalists, who spread word of tumult in a wider world.

Help students notice how political movements often borrow from each other, once again in a global framework. Students in the U.S., for example, may be interested to learn about the Polynesian Panthers, a liberation, activist, and community support group modeled on the American Black Panthers in California. Millenarian movements tied to religion and cargo across island Melanesia and independence conflicts between Papua and Indonesia all looked to history for inspiration. The idea of a Black Pacific traces the connections between, for example, activists in South Africa,

North America, and also in Australia and New Zealand. Have students think about the ways that, in some cases, "black" might refer to a cultural or historical alliance between African Americans and Australian Aboriginal peoples, or the Maori of Aotearoa/New Zealand and Native American tribal leaders. What leads one group to align with another? Is it based on common experiences, ideologies, or shared principles?

Think about Local Politics

From the era of formal French, British, and American Pacific colonialism, the narrative of history reaches to the 1970s and '80s, the rise of grassroots activism and indigenous Pacific Arts, the era of cultural flowering, and organizations dedicated to autonomy and community power as linked to wider pan-Pacific and pan-Asian identities. In Vanuatu, the proposal of "Kastom" (custom) reflects a search for alternative models of sovereignty that was also raised by Aboriginal, Kanak, Maori, and Hawaiian performative cultures. Unique (not exclusive, but still unique) narratives link Pacific Island decolonization to strong movements for local cultural preservation and custom. What this means is less emphasis on the more globally familiar chronicles of national liberation armies, guerilla movements, and perhaps male-dominated approaches to conceiving new nation-states on a territorial model. Rather, decolonization meant continuity of language, practice, and local self-determination, domains where women were particularly strong and active. Thinking through gendered political models can be quite instructive in these cases. How do students' own understandings of politics affect distinctions between male and female roles, or the appropriate actions, activities, or self-representations of women and men in leadership?[7] Why do some communities, or countries, have female leaders, while others do not?

Much of what can be understood as decolonization in the Pacific Islands, even historically, can readily be located away from the grand figures, decision makers, politicians, and military leaders that often dominate anticolonial studies. This is an opportunity to really discuss the way politics looks in many parts of the world: localized and neighborhood, town, or village oriented. Instead of speeches, conventions, and media broadcasts, politics often looks like women organizing dinners in their homes, meetings at local schools, formal and informal gatherings in churches with leaders, pastors, or chiefs. Politics also looks like activism — broadsides, placards, demonstrations, rallies, and protests for representation, sovereignty, or big causes — like antinuclear testing. Political history should represent the agitation of communities and peoples rather than only the machinations and strategies of leaders, rulers, and renowned figures. Work with students on these questions. Many of them may work as organizers for local political or social justice campaigns. Some may be volunteers or activists. How do they connect their neighborhood or community work with larger issues that may affect an entire population or nation?

Focus on Atomic Warfare as a Test Case

In many ways, one of the final acts of the Pacific War, the dropping of atomic bombs on Japan, heralded the next chapter of colonial dominance, anti-imperialist struggles, and sovereignty challenges in a Pacific defined by confrontations. Here we can think about a useful duality of the political and environmental in teaching: the violence of environmental depredations, from warfare to atomic testing to mining and overfishing — and the ways in which these actions were deeply connected to broader struggles for sovereignty, autonomy, and self-determination. In effect, anticolonial struggles began to reach critical mass.

The atomic bombings, as is well known, inaugurated a new era, one historically marked by a realization that the world could be annihilated by technological powers outstripping human understanding. That fear, however, was not only a generalized apprehension but a deadly reality for peoples of Asia and the Pacific. Though generations have now learned of the inconceivable suffering that would be caused by nuclear warfare, it is always well to remember that some have already experienced that directly. Japanese civilians became leaders of some of the most widespread international peace movements (or at least antinuclear movements) in history. Pacific Islanders from Bikini Atoll, Rongerik, and across the Marshall Islands were for decades exposed to, displaced by, and caused suffering by the literal and figurative fallout of American atomic testing in their islands.

CHAPTER SEVEN

Students can engage with these questions in many ways: through debating the military necessity of the bombs dropping on Japan, to the legacies of whether the action saved lives and deterred an invasion of the Japanese islands, to the question of the knowledge of radioactive sickness and ailments across generations, to the negligence or unconcern of American military and scientific establishment figures toward the destruction of island communities. In terms of the lasting legacies of atomic fallout, students are encouraged to view notable documentary films such as *Half Life*, or the award-winning *Radio Bikini*, which is almost entirely assembled from official U.S. government news footage, along with thought-provoking interviews. The effect of this is to see, formally, how a good filmmaker (Robert Stone) makes use of editing and juxtaposition, but also to hear and weigh whether sources deserve credibility or incredulity.[8] How do students today experience the reality (or unreality) of nuclear war and fallout possibilities? For students with global health interests, what do they understand medically about the effects of radiation exposure in the environment over generations?

Instructors and students may have long debates about this, and many scholarly works underscore the damage done across generations to local peoples as a function of atomic testing and environmental radioactive poisoning, but also through constant resettlement, restriction, and colonizing of island chains for military purposes with privileged settler colonies of military, administrative, and technical personnel supported by laborers from adjoining atolls. See the works of Jane Dibblin or Barbara Rose Johnston and Holly Barker.[9] It is critical to also understand the role that women such as Darlene Keju and Lijon Eknilang and women's organizations have played in antinuclear movements, perhaps because of moral and historical imperatives driven by the terror of radiation sickness and mutation in children yet unborn. Antinuclear protests became a global issue because testing issues—long a domain of the military and controlled by secrecy and official declarations—became a worldwide fear over contamination of the oceans and the global food supply, and the care of mothers for the next generation. Are there other global issues to which students are strongly attached? Think about environmental questions such as sustainability of food supplies and about climate change. Is the planet on a destructive course from which it can no longer turn back? Earlier generations have wrestled with such questions and taken action.

Other signal events in the antinuclear campaign help students understand how Islander groups aligned with an international network of peace activists and environmental groups in one of the most successful, broad-based coalitions in Pacific history, engaging independent states, former island colonies, and pacifist organizations from Japan to Europe and the United States. A standout moment to study is the French government's secret bombing of a protest ship — the *Rainbow Warrior* — in the harbor of Auckland, New Zealand, an international crime that is particularly noteworthy because the ship belonged to Greenpeace, the globally known environmental group. Many students are familiar with their campaigns. This is a good opportunity to discuss the tactics and limits of protests, direct confrontation, and attempts to shame and drive global opinion as forms of politics — and what the consequences sometimes are. It is also an excellent moment to note the ways that alliances form. The nuclear-free and independent Pacific movement was partly about antinuclear sentiment and agitation, but the "independent" part was also a global claim for indigenous authority and rights.

Connect Pacific Conflict to Environmental Issues

Other critical environmental issues include the results of overfishing. This kind of discussion is easy to materialize, as it can be raised from our dinner plates. Do the students eat canned tuna or other fish? Do they favor sushi? They can consider the importance placed on farmed, fresh, frozen, wild-caught, sustainably harvested, and so forth. Perhaps the key concept is to understand how commercial fishing fleets cost tens of thousands of dollars a day to operate and can, in capital terms, only afford to capture and keep the most marketplace-driven fish, that is, those that bring the best price. Nets, however, draw in all fish, and most are simply killed and dumped back into the oceans. The phenomenon of drift net fishing — now largely outlawed — is staggering to imagine.[10] In the 1970s, drift nets were tens of miles wide and scooped up everything in their mesh. To conceptualize this, students are encouraged to start from their own school and find a point up to thirty miles away as the size of a fishing net. Today, thinking through where a can of tuna comes from and how it is produced — from fishing fleet, to processing in a cannery often staffed by low-wage women in Asia or the Pacific Islands, then branding and marketing to worldwide consumers — is a study in itself. Do students think about where their everyday consumer items come from?

Not all of the challenges come from the sea. The Pacific is noted for mining, on islands like New Caledonia and Bougainville near the Solomons. In the latter, protests by women's groups against the destruction of the local environment by mining companies developed into armed warfare and years of violence that drew in local actors, guerilla fighters, mercenaries, and the troops of surrounding states. Students can note that large companies that extract resources regularly evoke mineral rights to resources far underground. Local villagers claim to own the land, but companies simply dig under them, leading to collapses, contamination, and poisoning of entire ecosystems, along with the social violence resulting from unstable and exploited populations of laborers.[11]

Debates using a town-hall model can be useful here, asking students to take positions favoring or opposing possible contracts with a large company, weighing the promise of jobs and development against future risks. This is an opportunity to discuss the ways that resource extraction can benefit populations — if it is sensitive to local conditions, and the value and gains are shared with local people, which rarely occurs. It can be quite a challenge for students to constitute themselves as a council or advisory board and come up with a plan that satisfies all. Every teaching context can include controversies known to students: Should pipelines be built? Should wells be drilled offshore? Who should get jobs and which industries should be given priority? Are some forms of energy or minerals valuable whereas others are not? Get specific: What about coal miners? Oil workers? "Fracking" for natural gas? What does it mean to base an economy on fossil fuels, as compared to renewable energy sources such as solar or wind or geothermal energy? Many students today are remarkably sophisticated in addressing these questions.

———— *Chapter Eight* ————

Identity as a Teaching Tool

Study How Groups and Individuals Define Themselves

In all of the cases in previous chapters, new historical identities are emerging, shaping new roles and images as sovereign peoples, cultural assertions of pride, economic and political autonomy, and new views of ethnic and religious minorities and majorities, as well as gender distinctions. The roles of women's activism, rights, and struggles for sovereignty have been pronounced. The overthrow of the Philippine government of Ferdinand Marcos in 1986 by a movement that became People Power under Corazon Aquino is a prominent historical case. Aquino was the widow of an assassinated political rival of the government who proved to be a formidable campaigner. Presenting herself as untainted by politics — while in fact a savvy strategist — she led a popular insurgent movement that captured power, excited admiration around the world (at least in the early years of her rule) and earned her Woman of the Year status.[1]

Students can study the many portrayals of Aquino in print, media, art, and words, shaping a visual identity for her as the female leader of an Asian country, and how this worked both for and against her as a woman who was also a politician. Her populist image proved powerful, even as she was often stymied by entrenched interests, and she drew authority from direct family and community activities that were traditionally assigned to women as mothers and protectors of children and homes. For whatever reason, however, it is unquestionable that major figures like Aquino, land activist Whina Cooper in Aotearoa/New Zealand, the Trask sisters in Hawai'i, female leaders protesting the Bougainville mine, and international women's congresses dedicated to popular interests, peace, and cooperative efforts began to significantly shape the politics of the Pacific. Where do students see evidence of women leaders around the world? Do they think that being male or female is a critical distinction in politics? Around what issues or commitments? Why does it appear more straightforward for women to be political leaders in some countries and more challenging in others?

Sovereignty and autonomy struggles cannot always be framed in ways customarily associated with men, such as armed insurgencies or nationalist movements. Newer forms of politics are engaging global issues such as health, the safety of children, educational opportunity, and the protection of families and the environment. As such they take on a different valence, significantly impacted by feminist movements and criticisms of unequal rights for males and females, even postindependence for many states. The poet and activist Grace Molisa openly wrote of domestic abuse and subordination of women in Vanuatu, even as the country was proclaiming its independence (for men). Scholars such as Margaret Jolly have given wide visibility to liberation that created freedoms for some, but not all.[2] In the Pacific, in fact, debate continues over the degree to which newly independent states built their social participation upon revived ideas of custom and tradition, precisely to counter the colonial imposition of capitalist, individualist modernity, while defining tradition as male-dominated political and social practices.

But were these customs truly ancestral, or were some—as with the Council of Great Chiefs in Fiji—actually themselves creations of colonial administrations, meant to assist in indirect rule by a favored few over communities of commoners? Were claims of male primacy in matters of decision making truly based on tradition, or impositions of contemporary interests, one party still seeking to control the other? Reading poems like Molisa's "Colonised People" for discussion can raise many issues about male and female power, abuse, and who truly carries the legacies of colonialism and of history.

For a powerful evocation of such themes, a novel that became a widely noted film, *Once Were Warriors*, based on the writings of the Maori author Alan Duff, is extraordinary and controversial, both for its raw sensibilities and for raising questions about whether it reinforced stereotypical images itself. A story of familial violence and abuse, the main narrative focuses on a strong woman for too long unable to find the means to confront her bullying husband, with consequences for her children. The sons and daughters—indeed all of the characters—each represent a way to confront and deal with a shared Maori past: through pride but slowness to act; through embracing a legendary heritage; by seeking an alternate family; by learning traditions; by rejecting what came before and trying to forget. In the end, the story is a searing lesson on the legacies of a fractured culture, and on what happens to those who struggle with or cannot come to terms with their own history.[3] How do students relate to their own personal histories? Are they of interest? What does genealogy mean beyond family reunions and time spent with grandparents? How much of "identity" comes from a shared sense of an ancestral past?

In addition to literary works, pay special attention to contemporary music—a subject students always enjoy. For example, the stirring and unique research of musicologist Gabriel Solis focuses on connections, influences, and differences marking combinations of indigenous instrumentation, funk, rock, and reggae in Australia and Papua New Guinea. Groups such as Yothu Yindi, No Fixed Address, Black Brothers, or Sanguma provide frameworks for musical expression that regularly address colonial, legal, and social injustices, pay homage to Bob Marley and Marcus Garvey, make use of bamboo flutes and log drums, and engage with questions of blackness and both local and global political consciousness. What other artists do students know, and how can they interpret their work historically, not just in terms of popular culture?[4]

Question Whether Justice Can Be Found in History

As noted above, many of the historical currents of the post–Pacific War era are either framed or driven by broad anticolonial movements. These movements began to ask troubling questions about the relationship between the past and their own lived present. Some of these are directly political confrontations, while others manifest in claims and agitation for rights, recognition, and equal standing. Certainly, the later decades of the twentieth century saw an efflorescence of cooperative charters, resolutions, and declarations, engaging everything from antinuclear principles, to the protection of indigenous knowledge and property, to sovereignty and self-determination for subject peoples across the Pacific. Some notable movements have sought to come to terms with the past: the recognition of the Stolen Generation in Australia and the institutionalization of Sorry Day as an attempt to reflect on misbegotten policies designed to hasten the extinction of Aboriginal peoples by taking their children to be raised by others. Doris Pilkington's *Follow the Rabbit-Proof Fence*, which recounts her own family's separation, was made into a widely praised dramatic film.[5]

In Asia, women forced into sexual slavery by the Japanese Imperial Army continue to seek redress, and apologies, nonapologies, and demands for reparations have captured attention across generations. The question of war and war crimes responsibilities is ever present, fueling powerful discussions with students. The subject profoundly underscores the importance of historical consciousness and the truism that "the past is not past." Take time to have students discuss or debate the central question of whether justice, redress, reparations, or reconciliation can truly be effective. One can look, especially, to global debates about genocide legacies, from the Holocaust in Europe, to Rwanda, to the Turks and Armenians, and to questions about reparations and redress for Aboriginal societies in Australia, First Peoples in Canada, Native Americans in the U.S., or descendants of the transatlantic slave trade in South America, the Caribbean, and the United States.[6] Students may very well be familiar with controversies about slave owners who founded today's great American universities, and how their legacies should be addressed now. Have the students' own schools dealt with changing building names, returning donations, taking down monuments, or otherwise thinking about the power of historical memory?

In Asia and the Pacific, such controversies especially include Japan's role in the Pacific War—for example, the Rape of Nanjing, and the slavery and violation of the comfort women. The question of unrepentant militarism in Japan was revived in the 1970s by the phenomenon of straggler soldiers emerging from the jungle, who did not know, or did not believe, that World War II had ended almost thirty years before. Such cases are particularly compelling, and you should use them to raise issues about historical justice. The most famous straggler soldier was Hiroo Onoda, who came out of the Philippines, declaring that he had never been relieved of duty and so carried on long after Japan had surrendered, had been occupied, and was developed as a major industrial global power. By reappearing, he raised the memory of the war. His supporters saw him as the archetypal loyal samurai warrior; his detractors questioned what they saw as his blind loyalty to the emperor and his fanatical attachment to a discredited imperial ideology. Through such figures, students have a singular opportunity to understand not only what drives their actions, but how blame, responsibility, or justice can be attached to the memory of the past.[7] What war heroes or war generations are controversial in the students' own experience?

Asia was not the only part of the Pacific embroiled in questions about crimes and demands for redress. In the United States, President Bill Clinton apologized for the American seizure of the Hawaiian Kingdom and promised redress, though he did not agree to return the islands to the Hawaiian Kanaka Maoli people. Some scholar-activists have pitted Hawaiian sovereignty claims against the history of abuse and subordination by the U.S.—an imperial power against a Pacific nation. In such cases, demands for apologies and reparations raise the question whether justice can be gained from revisiting past events.[8] Every year, I have had students deeply committed to studying sovereignty movements—there are many—and have charged them to consider which positions they favor and why.

Should territories be divided? How should benefits be distributed and traditions protected? Should there be complete separation and secession?

Historians often focus on national identity—that is, how political and nation-state histories are used to decide how to define a people, and who is included or excluded. This is true around the world, from the Frenchness of the French being contested by younger Muslim generations, to the valorized mestizo ideologies of a Euro-Indian-African Brazil, the essentialist ideas behind the Han Chinese and Yamato Japanese, or the melting-pot narrative of the United States. Indigenous communities can also evoke a national perspective, as with the demands to restore the Hawaiian nation, or the First Nations Peoples of Canada.

Sometimes separatists seek to divide territories with common cultures but different claims to political legitimacy, as in China and Taiwan, South Korea and North Korea, or the multiple Islander groups included in the nation of Kiribati. Indigenous communities often resist the idea of a nation, focusing more on the continuity of cultural groups and seeking to preserve distinctive traditions, practices, knowledge, and languages within the context of a broader state, such as Aboriginal communities in Australia, or Native Americans in the United States. Students should engage with these questions: What do they think constitutes a legitimate claim? How should smaller communities and larger national identities coexist? Does one authority—whether political or cultural—have primacy over the other?

In the Pacific, these questions can be considered in terms of a Pacific Way, a claim that Island culture is unique. Political and cultural transformations are proposed based upon consultation with members of local kin and allied groups, a respect for elder generations, and a community built on obligations and shared responsibilities. Increasingly, it underscores the role of connections and mobility, most importantly and strikingly articulated by the Tongan writer and scholar Epeli Hauʻofa, whose essay "Our Sea of Islands" changed the idea of the Pacific from a place of empty water and small, isolated islands to one of vast networks of trade, alliance, kinship, and ancient histories tied to contemporary travel, where the sea itself is less a barrier than a highway or corridor integrating the entire world.[9] His work is a necessary touchstone for all teachers and Pacific scholars.

PART III

Performed Histories

———— *Chapter Nine* ————

Distinguish Representations and Realities

See the Differences between Experience and Image

A clear theme emerges when discussing how histories might be told after the mid-twentieth century: many of the historical currents of the post–Pacific War era are framed or driven by the legacies of the conflict. There are numerous ways to get at these questions, but a couple that are highly salient are the phenomenon known as the cargo cult, and the global industry of tourism. These are oddly complementary, in that both trade in representations of other cultures and how best to exploit that engagement with the exotic and unknown. Also, both not only are representations of the world, but are heavily dependent upon performing what they purport to describe. Students should be prepared to consider how particular representations are historically specific; that is, they respond to particular times and issues (decolonization, global modernization) while — in many cases — rehearsing some very old stories, such as the first encounter between advanced and supposedly primitive worlds; a longing and a search for a paradisiacal, or innocent and uncontaminated, people.

Especially noted in Melanesian islands like Tanna, the cargo cult is characterized by a fascination of local villagers with material goods from the outside world and a ritualized set of practices, including marching and military-style drilling, intended to solicit the arrival or return of an iconic figure—John Frum—based on an apocryphal American GI, "John from...," who brought with him great wealth in the form of "cargo."[1]

Parts of the history of the phenomenon are not hard to trace—during the Pacific War, Islanders were, indeed, astounded by the extraordinary number of men, landing craft, shipments, and containers that came ashore, often producing entire compounds equipped with motor pools, hospitals, kitchens, barracks, and entertainment in the jungle. This appearance of material wealth in the context of warfare and savage conflict shaped a vision of a changed world, which indeed it was, to which John Frum would return one day to proclaim a new order. To those who find this cult-like behavior more than a little curious, followers of John Frum can only note that Christians seem to have been waiting more than two thousand years for the return of their savior, with much less material promise and evidence. Do students think that stories or dogmas from their own faiths might look strange to others? Which parts can be discussed, and which parts simply cannot be questioned?

As scholars like Lamont Lindstrom have pointed out, the obsession with cargo, often attributed to cultists, seems in reality much less an Islander fixation than a Western desire to see supposedly primitive peoples enraptured by modern appliances. This is a good place for you to engage students with questions or exercises related to their own everyday lives. In what ways do they participate in commodity and consumer culture? How many of them fetishize the latest fashion, electronics, or status gadgets (the smart phone is the most obvious example)? To what degree do the students find themselves obsessed with or addicted to their devices, and how have they oriented their lives and identities around the lifestyle promised by the device?

It is then useful to understand the cargo phenomenon reflected in oneself, and also to see how community movements in the Oceanian islands, far from being quaint, in fact had very historically situated meanings. That is, they had all of the elements of anticolonial consciousness. Indeed, John Frum meetings became an alternate form of very local worship, emptying out traditional churches and challenging institutional religion in the islands with pragmatic, messianic visions of an alternative future. In this way, the cargo cult is in many respects a form of cultural and national liberation politics, and its apparent strangeness lies in the modern world's desire to believe in savages who think that foreigners are somehow gods.

Understand How the Primitive Is Represented

Similarly, it is very interesting to teach about such questions through the lens of the Tasaday people in the Philippines. Few students today will remember this first- or even secondhand, but the supposed discovery in the 1970s of a small clan of cave-dwelling "primitives" who lived by foraging and had no apparent contact with others generated worldwide curiosity and excitement. These were purportedly Stone Age people living untouched, possibly for millennia, speaking no known language, never having seen machines, and doing work with handmade stone tools. Debate soon raged about how old the Tasaday were — and could they possibly truly be survivors from an earlier age in human history? The story became even more fraught when researchers began to note inconsistencies in Tasaday culture — why were there no typical refuse heaps (middens) or epic narrative tales? The mystery deepened when the Philippine government closed off all access or contact with them, and the debates exploded when, a decade later, a journalist came back from the rain forest with a stunning story: he claimed the Tasaday were a hoax — local villagers paid off to act like primitives for the benefit of anthropologists, camera crews, and global media.[2]

This is an incredible case to teach. Were the Tasaday really Stone Age peoples, living in peace and harmony with nature? Were they pretenders, hired by the government to attract favorable attention to local indigenous policy, invite donations, and claim large tracts of resource-rich land as government reserves? Some Tasaday suggested they were pretending;

others insisted they were real; sometimes a single individual would change stories depending on who was asking. The key question is, as with the cargo cult, How much of this story depends on a Western yearning to discover supposedly untouched and primitive peoples? How much of it reflects the desire of local rain forest communities to be left alone, play roles, or change with the times as they themselves saw fit? In all cases, consider the Heisenberg uncertainty principle of history: real or not, once contact was made, it became impossible to know what an untouched people would look like, since observation itself changed all subsequent actions.

Teach the Importance of Tourism

One of the key ways that a vision of uncontaminated Pacific peoples has been elaborated is not through anthropological discovery, but through the commodity-marketing strategies of tourism. Across the globe, many histories can be comprehensively told without ever mentioning tourism, but not in the Pacific. Touristic representations of Oceania and Asia are so strong that they have become standard descriptions of entire regions and peoples. From the Orient of mystery and exoticism to the palm trees and sandy beaches of a Polynesian paradise, the Pacific has been thoroughly redescribed as a place of adventure and idyll.

In fact, this is a very accessible and often popular way to develop exercises and discussions with students: have them bring in, show off, or just talk about the touristic representations and stereotypes of a particular people or place and what they do in terms of describing, yet also shaping, local histories. Consider Pacific Islanders with flowers in their hair, smiling or dancing in colorful costume — usually young women — or Asian markets, elders, and, overlayered, more complex clichés, like the sampan in Hong Kong harbor, or the skyscraper adjacent to the Buddhist temple.

Tourism is a highly visual study, and students can discuss and interpret many types of images, from the romance of postcards to kitschy copies of native apparel, icons, totems, and instruments. Most historians today can work extensively with material culture objects and also with the ideological histories embedded in postcards, posters, travel books, and cinematic representations.[3] It is also interesting to study the ways that particular businesses market entire regions, for example the pineapple or sugar growers with their staged images of farmers, or pinup girls to represent lush, agricultural islands.

It is critical to recognize tourism as not just a representational strategy or purveyor of marketable cultural experiences, but as an industry — in fact, one of the largest in the world, encompassing vast realms of transport, lodging, hospitality, food service, performers, entertainers, guides, and artists, both domestic and international. It is always engaging and helpful to use a case study, and the Polynesian Cultural Center on the island of Oahu in Hawai'i is exemplary.[4] As an attraction that includes a wide range of island villages modeled on different cultures, each staffed with folkloric islanders dancing, engaging in traditional crafts, and sharing stories and legends, it allows examination of multiple issues.

Whether one sees this as a splendid example of cultural preservation and transmission of island heritage or an exploitative theme park is exactly the question. Examining or watching images of warriors dancing, tourists drifting across an artificial lagoon, or a Las Vegas–style Polynesian luau show raises many questions about how tourism works as the selling of culture. A point worth noting is that everyone is pleasant and happy, so if this is history, it is largely one that excludes change or political struggle. You can easily engage students by asking where they have traveled. What did they see and what did it mean? Are they aware of being presented particular images, or did they believe themselves to be seeing real life? Do these distinctions even make any sense? How is tourism a very particular way of experiencing the world?

It is helpful to propose to students that tourism is an industry trading in managed experiences, and that behind those experiences and created expectations labors a complex and mobile workforce, constantly struggling to earn a living in the context of picturesque landscapes. In the modern era this is reflected in Oceanian flight and migration — the movement of Melanesian islanders to Australian plantations, South Asian Indians to Fiji, Japanese to Hawai'i, Hawaiians to the Pacific Northwest, or Filipinos and Chinese across the world. This movement of peoples can be studied not only in terms of labor, but by joining labor questions to those of political or cultural persecution, and engaging with the issue of refugee populations.

Understand Mobility as Forced Displacement

Thousands of Vietnamese fled their homeland after the victory of the North over the South in the 1970s. Desperate families set out in overcrowded water craft hoping to reach other parts of Southeast or East Asia, or Australia. Students might be asked if they know the term "boat people," which originated then. In recent decades, questions of refugee boats have continued to challenge policy makers and national governments in Australia, where Central Asian families have sought asylum by way of Indonesian islands and have been detained in offshore camps.[5] This has also taken place in Europe, which many have tried to reach after fleeing Syria and North Africa. Innumerable news accounts and a growing body of oral history and testimonial literature are available to help students gain insights into these events.

In contemporary situations, what outsiders see as exotic or picturesque natives might be supporting families in trades as farm, factory, or domestic workers. In fact, a particular way to engage students with the idea of transnational labor is to focus on workers that they may or may not notice around them. These can include the workforce that often supports their own institutions of education—from custodial staff, to dining or food service personnel, groundskeepers, or even child care workers. Detailed and personalized cases can be strikingly revealing. How much are students aware of laborers and workers around them? How much are such individuals and communities invisible to them? Are the students themselves part of this labor force, and how do they experience that?

In my classes, I examine the life of an ordinary woman, Flor Contemplacion. A Filipina nanny with her own family to support who worked in Singapore for a Chinese family to earn money to send home, Contemplacion was accused of drowning her client's child, and then was convicted and hanged by the government. Some said she had been framed by her employer because as a low-paid, overseas worker she was effectively defenseless, and almost all agreed that she was part of an exploitative global system whereby the poor of one country were forced to migrate to support their own families by working in another part of the world, often under abusive, and certainly unprotected, conditions. Her execution resulted in broken diplomatic relations, international debates, and a dramatic film re-creation of her case.[6] Students have an opportunity to reflect on the often invisible economy and how—depending upon one's perspective— it provides opportunities, allows unwanted immigration by foreigners, or relentlessly exploits and abuses vulnerable workers with few other opportunities to improve their own lives.

The lesson in considering immigration (or refugees), whether from Latin America into the United States, from Central Asia and North Africa into the European Union, from Southeast Asia into East Asia, from islands to continents and vice versa is that anywhere labor is needed, prejudices and marginalization are strong. Students can weigh in with their own views, ideas, and preconceptions. Are foreigners a threat? Do they take away jobs from locals? Do they help build communities? Do new customs and beliefs threaten local identities? Are there, or should there be, humanitarian obligations?

Relate to Contemporary Politics

The Pacific region is also embroiled in global debates about state violence and terrorism, by both organized groups and national governments. The Philippines remain a test case, where deep histories dating from original human settlement and later Catholic dominance have shaped an archipelago that is governed from Manila in the name and interests of the Christian north, while rebel forces in the south have agitated for generations for greater autonomy and rights as a Muslim polity. Military conflicts between government troops and the Moro National Liberation Front have led to extended violence, displacement of populations, and claims and counterclaims of outrages, atrocities, crimes, and terrorism.

The horrific bombing of a tourist nightclub on the island of Bali, resulting in the death of scores of Australians, troubled relations between Australia and Indonesia. This took place shortly after the attack on the World Trade Center in New York City in 2001, thus tying together distant locales into what political leaders in the United States and Europe called a global war on terror. Kidnapping and ransom organizations like Abu Sayyaf, operating in Southeast Asian seas, have also been declared terroristic, though it is less clear whether they are ideologically driven or criminally opportunistic. In 2019, the mass shooting of Muslim worshippers at a mosque in Christchurch, New Zealand, and then a series of coordinated bombings of Christian communities in Sri Lanka each claimed scores of victims. The scale of bloodshed left the world reeling, with investigators and commentators seeking motivations in distorted or extremist political and religious beliefs. Students can readily engage with their own views on the role of government in providing security for citizens, and the limits and possibilities of combating terrorism carried out by groups that have no defined government to attack.[7] What is terrorism? What about "domestic terrorism?" Are these distinctive phenomena, or the same? Who defines them, and in what cases do the labels apply, and in what cases not? Which threats are real? Which are exaggerated? How should governments respond? How will better historical and cultural knowledge generate better understandings for answering these questions?

───── *Chapter Ten* ─────

See the Process of Enacting Knowledge

Engage with Environmental Histories

The philosophy called the Pacific Way — respecting traditions and elders, working by consensus, negotiating differences — is a resonant form of cultural politics, but it has also been more broadly engaged through issues that impact the natural world, particularly in tracing the profound impacts of global changes on Islander and coastal peoples, including climate change, sea-level change, and the environmental disaster of disappearing islands and aquifers contaminated by saltwater. These are clearly global matters with which most students will be familiar. While the mechanisms of climate change continue to be debated — and do encourage students to explore multiple positions — the effects of the earth's warming are indisputably on display in the melting of polar ice and the submersion of low-lying atolls in the Indian Ocean and in the Pacific, notably in Kiribati.

Pacific Island nations are regionally united to advocate for seriously addressing environmental issues. Work with students to convey that, for many Islanders, sea-level change and stronger storms are not just scientific theories or political positions. The effects are neither speculative nor projected into the future, but are manifesting now as vanished territory. Salt pans are forming on land, and coastal damage and erosion from both rising sea levels and the greater energy of warm water in tropical storms are increasing. Are students aware that former islands are now submerged?

This discussion of real situations can take the form of a debate, including the pros and cons of climate change policy — the responsibilities of the industrial and developing worlds, the questions of economic productivity and preservation, destruction of coral and fish stocks, and pollution of the oceans.[1] Concern for environmental protection in the Pacific and an adherence to natural cycles and limits are not folkloric but deeply tied to contemporary debates about sustainability and appropriate stewardship of natural resources. Students can be readily engaged in discussions of effective global warming policy, which can be structured around the complexity of trying to negotiate agreements, whether carbon restrictions, cap-and-trade, or taxation of carbon emissions as means to address an issue that no nation can address alone — only global agreements and cooperation will have any effect. Ask students, why is it so hard to make such agreements? How do individual governments or nations make a case for themselves as an exception, or in opposition? As a classic question, what would students themselves, individually, be willing to give up in terms of their own comforts or convenience in order to address such big issues?

Challenge students to consider how development, pollution, and energy use in one part of the world can multiply climate change effects in another. Different parts of the Pacific are connected through political and environmental hazards. The catastrophic Tohoku earthquake and tsunami off the coast of Japan in 2011 is a case in point, not only for its tragic loss of life and devastation, but in its implications for nuclear energy policy and wider environmental contamination from failed reactors, the loss of surrounding farmland, and the eerie appearance of wreckage around the Pacific, including debris that drifted all the way to the northwestern coast of the United States.

You will find it valuable to have students think about the Pacific region as both very localized — different islands, coastal nations, and peoples — yet also interconnected. As in the Tohoku quake, effects in one place create changes in another. Changing weather patterns and warming water in the southern ocean may divert or kill off local fish species, thus causing cascading effects up the food chain all the way to Canada. You can highlight particular species — whales, deep-sea tuna, birds like the sooty shearwater — and the ways they traverse thousands of miles, connecting what is for them a truly Pacific world.[2] Ask students how well-known phenomena such as birds flying south or sea turtles returning to the place where they were born illustrate the interconnectedness of the natural world.

Explain the Pacific Century

Teaching about the Pacific today necessarily reckons with the question of a Pacific modernity, or even a postmodernity, especially in the complicated and often ill-defined language describing the contemporary Pacific, generated by scholars or continental policy makers or ideologues. The idea of the Pacific Rim, that the area bounded by Asia and the Americas is destined to become the center of the twenty-first-century world, resonates strongly.[3] That is, the locus of political and economic power is shifting from Europe to Asia, framed by emerging and emergent economies known as the Asian Tigers, including Singapore, Malaysia, and Taiwan and led by China and Japan.

This idea of Pacific leadership dates back to at least the nineteenth century and the Western recognition of the vast opportunities for engagement in (and, at that time, conquest of) East Asia — hence the American opening of Japan, the partition of China, the French empire in Laos, Cambodia, and Vietnam as Indochina, along with early modern empires of the Dutch in Indonesia and the Spanish in the Philippines. In the postwar period, Japan's remarkable economic miracle became a model for Asian development, along with the success of the capitalist city-state of Singapore under Prime Minister Lee Kuan Yew. The Japanese case is especially useful, for students in any part of the world can easily name any number of Japanese multinational brands and describe their products:

from Toyota and Mitsubishi to Sony and Panasonic, to Mazda, Canon, Nikon, Honda, Nissan, Hitachi, and a dozen more.[4] Usually, fewer can name Chinese companies, even though China has a larger economy — a testament to a developing nation that achieved strong capitalist name recognition.

Students should recognize that these brands and products are part of a deliberate, and much emulated, export-driven national economic model, and that they reflect a key historical question: the ways that particular countries deal with the past and present by providing a national model of the future. In fact, the question of generations is very keen in Japan, where youth culture is organized around a hyper-postmodern vision of a rapidly transforming society, straddling both tradition and modernity.

This is generally very easy to teach, as most students are knowledgeable about, and even obsessed by, Japanese popular culture, particularly the graphic stylings of manga and anime — the famous graphic novels and animated movies. In this case, just ask students for their favorites and what they might mean, or hunt for classics such as the cyberpunk apocalypse of *Akira* or the legacies of war detailed in *Grave of the Fireflies*, or the superpower longings and contests of serials like *Dragonball* or *Bleach*, or the object lessons and ingrained cuteness of the Pokémon franchise — and the commercial commodity empire of Hello Kitty.[5]

Other ways to teach global history as Pacific history include the everyday and the highly abstract, from food customs to trade policy. Students often enjoy studying, researching, and thinking about different regional cuisines. How do national cultures define what is Polynesian food, or Chinese, Japanese, or Vietnamese? You can engage questions of style, savor, and spice but also raise an interesting premise: an examination of food safety and security in the Pacific region. The production, distribution, and administration of food, ranging from meeting basic needs, to social welfare programs, to agribusiness and public health have coalesced in recent years into formidable areas of study.

Food disputes can be a rich source of thinking about global Pacific and Asian and American debates. Will this involve largely policy questions? Tariff and trade agreements? Ocean issues like overfishing, or tropical cash cropping? Have students heard of Golden Rice, which has been bioengineered to provide additional nutrients to undernourished populations? Advocates hail it as a great advance in public health. Opponents say it destroys local small farms and their indigenous crops and is yet another example of unwanted genetically modified organisms in the food chain. Most students have opinions on GMOs, for health or political reasons.[6]

Likewise, global institutions can be studied in terms of the transfer of administrative knowledge and practice: nations regularly compare themselves in terms of political and social administration. One might, for example, think about transposing the New Zealand model of assistance to poor single mothers to Canada: What social, political, or ideological configurations frame decisions, and what makes New Zealand's model attractive? This is important for students to learn, for just like commercial popular culture, diffusionist models often wrongly suggest that only dominant key centers (like the United States) radiate policy and ideas and products. This is so flatly wrong that it needs correction with examples, especially less well-known ones, of how polities borrow from each other.

Raise the China Question

China is a great example of a challenge to Western industrial eminence. Of course, China can and should be discussed in terms not only of Chinese history, but of the continuing and increasingly assertive role of the Chinese state in the Pacific. The main point here is that though China needs to be reckoned as a rising power, Chinese impact is nothing new, and that from Zheng He's Treasure Fleets to the Manila galleon transits, to diasporic labor communities and cross-lateral engagements during and after the Pacific War, China's Pacific presence is more a rediscovery than a new phenomenon. The ambitious Silk Road Economic Belt and the twenty-first-century Maritime Silk Road initiatives announced in 2013 by Chinese president Xi Jinping are worth discussing. The combined project would become known as the Belt and Road Initiative or, more popularly, the New Silk Road, an enormous infrastructure of transport and communication links that would stretch from China across Central Asia to Europe. The evocation of the ancient routes and the ambition to extend Chinese economic, political, cultural — and military — influence are clearly evident, leading to consternation in Europe and the United States as well as across Asia. Providing students with such contexts that link the past, present, and future is obligatory for anyone thinking about China's geostrategic role.

China means the People's Republic, but also — depending upon your focus — Taiwan, diasporic communities, and minorities in the Pacific Islands, with a dizzying array of both strong and weak ties to a home country — sometimes real, sometimes only a pragmatic fiction. Taiwan has increasingly embraced an Austronesian narrative as part of its heritage, in a clear effort to make a claim for Taiwan as an Oceanian and Pacific-oriented China, historically distinct from the Han-centric China of the People's Republic.

To talk about China, one must underscore the multiple registers and constantly evolving nature of Chinese community and influence building around the Pacific and the world, from the rural Chinese to the urban, intermixed, and intermarried communities that have often been seen as interlopers and targeted for discrimination, yet who have also integrated strongly and helped to power local economies. Is there any urban center in the world without some sort of Chinatown? Ask students about the ways they have interacted with Chinese influence — whether through personal family connections, consumer goods, diasporic communities, travel, or the electronic components in their smartphones. These are good points to underscore and are widely discussed in contemporary journalism.

Some of these points may seem self-evident, yet it is also striking how much attention is paid in popular parlance to China or China's role, as if such a singular entity actually existed. Any reader seeking a primer on the major arguments about the current generation would be rewarded with a quick overview of major scholars on the China/Pacific question, from Ron Crocombe to Terence Wesley-Smith, Tara Kabutalaka, Jian Yang, Ed Porter, Graeme Smith, Wang Gungwu, and a host of others from the University of Hawaiʻi at Mānoa and the Australian National University especially, debating the ideas of an arc of instability, local elites, domestic versus international strategic entanglements, and the key roles of nonstate actors in defining in terms of receptivity to aid donation politics on a Pacific-wide scale.[7] Consider also how major antigovernment protests in Hong Kong, especially in 2018–19, underscore tensions of new and old generations coming into conflict about social, political, and—especially—economic issues.

You may also find it useful to note the definition of China as a polity when paired with Asian neighbors, as these are contentious issues: note the concern about Chinese economic and political power and the tensions around Chinese territorial claims and the construction of artificial islands around the Scarborough Shoal and the Senkaku or Diaoyu Islands, and other maritime disputes as impacting perceptions at least of island politics—particularly as tied to resources. In the first decades of the twenty-first century, China's development of military installations in the South China Sea and the relentless dredging and sand-deposit building of new island territories around atolls formerly almost submerged have generated questions of whether a geopolitical shift is underway, displacing the Atlantic world in favor of the Pacific.

This has revived intense review of Chinese history in the Pacific. Of special interest are Chinese leadership roles in the Pacific Islands, including figures such as Julius Chan, Anote Tong, Gaston Tong Sang, and Jim Ah Koy, and early seafaring links, as well as older and newer generations of migrants, immigrants, and sojourners. The key points are the rediscovered engagement of the Chinese with the Pacific (i.e., this is deeply historic, not a newly globalized Pacific Rim phenomenon) and that Chinese communities are so widespread that they integrate incredible diversity in terms of cultural and ethnic qualities, regional backgrounds (Fujien, Hokkien especially), economic statuses, and political allegiances (Taiwan, the People's Republic, the Philippines, Indonesia). Again, there is no China as a singular entity. More attention must be paid to social and diasporic histories, as well as the multiplicities of nonstate actors, agents, migrants, and travelers, that is, less focus on China as a political and strategic monolith or mystery.

A history built up from the claims of particular communities rather than by beginning with the statist approach reads differently. This challenges the idea of China as merely a great power by refocusing not on China but on Chineseness: as historian Paul D'Arcy puts it, "Does being a small fragmented group in a foreign land lead members to seek identity and security in a collective 'Chinese' identity or to retreat to the mainstays of Chinese life, family and local community identity?"[8]

What is salutary here is that these questions could be asked of almost any diasporic or ethnically or culturally defined people. There is no particularity about the China question. Yet such generalities are, as always, inflected by their histories. For example, the previously mentioned Austronesian renaissance in Taiwan is very particular to the ways that indigenous qualities are asserted through cultural pride and historical rediscovery, and framed by a triangular reckoning between China, Taiwan, and indigenous Islanders. The effect is a distancing of "Chinese" identity from the mainland, with a concomitant alliance with Oceania and Southeast Asia. Overall, it is especially intriguing to work with national perspectives: that is, depending on where the instruction is taking place, how are the Chinese perceived in general media and news—whether you are in Europe, North America, Japan, Singapore, Fiji, Indonesia, Australia, or New Zealand? What stereotypes and prejudices, or points of admiration, respect, and unease do you see? All of these underscore the complexity of defining China: the critical literature around Chineseness and Chinese diasporic communities around the world and the particularities of the People's Republic, Taiwan, overseas, and indigenous interplays and tensions.

Ask Who Tells the Story

One of the great scholarly disputes is the question of who speaks on behalf of peoples and communities. Who tells the story of a people, and what does it mean for a people to be telling their own story? This can be a long and complicated discussion. Do we own our own stories? To what degree are we indebted to our culture, our family, our national organization, to authorities? It's important to define who is a legitimate or authentic spokesperson. In some cases—such as the comfort women—the victims make individual claims for justice. Can justice for the past be had? What if the aggrieved are a group, historically? Thus, debates lead to claims about greater classes of victims — a community, a culture, a people. Parallel cases also resonate, such as the role of entire communities and the place of women in Okinawa, in the historic Ryukyu Islands, for centuries part of Japan and the more recent site of U.S. military bases, with constant tensions over military and civilian relations, cases of sexual abuse, and an economy tied to serving military interests and personnel.

Students can certainly debate this, particularly in terms of making claims on behalf of particular ethnic, cultural, racial, or underrepresented groups. Students are often keen to recognize how contemporary expansions of perspective — via the internet, social media, and electronic communications — have allowed any individual to tell a story and present her or his own facts and interpretations. Which are credible, reliable, and trustworthy?

It can be engaging to discuss how cultural histories are maintained, controlled, and appropriated. Comparing multiple accounts from different media about controversial cases, as above, is highly instructive. For specific examples, think about first-contact narratives, stories of genocide and survival, war crimes, victimization and perpetrators, responsibility for climate change, atomic bombings, sexual slavery, or personal identity. Who tells these stories, and then what debates arise as different parties disagree about the meaning and interpretation of the past?[9] At a more scholarly level, Pacific-wide and interconnected research can focus on particular cases as institutions tell their stories — always helpful with student research.

You could focus on how museums use preservation discourses, then cite examples of the ways that revitalization projects can affect communities. This allows museums to be actors rather than repositories and has promise in breaking away from more familiar representational critical museum studies. Studying institutions comparatively from Fiji to the Barbados points up the way that Pacific Islanders and those of the Caribbean often find common cause.[10]

Along the same lines, the anthropological discourse that indigenous peoples are disappearing and will become culturally and historically extinct, especially through disease and ruinous contact with civilization, needs interrogation. Here, the notable contribution is not the articulation of that idea — which will be familiar to scholars — but to correct it by underscoring the living nature of supposedly vanished cultures. For example, you could focus on Tasmania and Tierra del Fuego. This is truly a South-South examination, organized around peoples who are already perceived as marginalized through their geographical location. Examining similar beliefs about such cultures is important, using the narratives of living inhabitants as critical evidence.

Likewise, historical cases involving the repatriation of human remains held in research institutions raises fraught questions that are always entangled with matters of institutional knowledge, cultural heritage, and struggles over conservatorship and guardianship, not to mention memory and politics. Aboriginal remains in Australian collections, or those of Hawaiian/Kanaka Maoli in Hawai'i are key examples. Certainly, the function of bodies as specimens in scholarly institutions is important (e.g., what justifications were given?), and elucidating the legal claims requires contract, policy, and exchange histories in parallel cases. When should remains be scientific specimens? When are they revered ancestors that should be returned for burial? What conditions should be negotiated? How would students feel if remains of their own family members were held as scientific specimens?[11]

Geography also matters. A particular focus on Australia and Latin America in such cases can force students to think of a new East and West that is not primarily about North America and East Asia. Equally, Australia and Mexico and Central America can be thematically and geographically resonant when studying museums and scientific collections and the controversies that arise around them.

These discussions are all about biopolitics in a certain way, and are thematically about displacement and the collision of a technical world with indigenous cultures, and the search for legitimate forms of indigenous expression and assertion. Students might find it fascinating to discuss how they themselves are identified by biological traits, in relation to the work of Kehaulani Kauanui, who has devoted considerable scholarship to studying the question of blood quantum in defining who is really a Hawaiian. The issue — tied as it is to particular rights, recognitions, and financial entitlements — has high stakes for many communities. Analogous debates occur in Native American communities about who properly has Indian blood, and how it is defined, as a marker and often as a key factor in whether someone can claim membership in a particular tribal group.[12]

Another popular way to get at personal histories is through engaging short films such as *Made in Taiwan*, in which friends and media personalities, one of Samoan heritage and the other Maori, decide to submit their DNA to a testing service and then go on a peripatetic adventure across island chains, and — by implication — back through history, to find the linkages across generations that indicate primary ancestors from Taiwan, thus affirming the narrative of Austronesian-Polynesian heritage. How many students have done their own consumer DNA testing, or ancestry tracing, with all of the attendant promises to reveal exciting details about personal heritage? Are they willing to share these results? Why has this form of popular genealogy become so popular — and such a big business? What does it say about wanting to connect with ancestors?

Plan for Testing and Exams

Of course, teaching Pacific histories through "enacting knowledge" and "making their own histories" is not only an assertion of voice, agency, or reckoning with historical actors, but a commentary on what students might gain from such encounters, and how that knowledge might be rightly assessed. In terms of the staples of classroom teaching — instruction and exams — a wide variety of engagements are possible.

From the beginning of this primer, every other paragraph or so I have raised questions derived from the materials and subjects under study. Some of these are specific to the evidence or inquiry at hand; many more are general in nature, about the students' own experiences, and how they can relate their lives to the discussions. The idea here is not only to engage the students in learning Pacific histories — though that is obviously the primary goal — but to see themselves as historical figures too, participating in the creation of knowledge. I have mentioned numerous specific exercises, including the study of artifacts and illustrations and the adoption of different analogies for scholarly study: working like an archaeologist to piece together material evidence and extrapolate lifeways, and survival and navigation systems; or engaging with anthropology to draw on the insights of linguistics and cultural forms from kinship to ritual power.

Genealogy and molecular biology, as well as tools like carbon dating and DNA sampling, have allowed researchers to posit the routes of ancestors and the transmission of lineages and their goods, and these tools have themselves been popularized for the public. We have discussed how histories are also transmitted through performances and creative actions, not just archives and documents. Especially in Oceanian cultures, understanding performed expressions of the past requires curiosity about dance, music, and the plastic arts such as sculpture, as well as oratorical forms.

The lecture format is efficient, but make sure to populate your presentations with extensive visuals, as many students will have little familiarity with the appearances of peoples, places, and times under discussion. For standard exams, brief responses identifying key materials paired with comparative and thematic essays provide a good balance. Brief responses can consist of identifying key concepts in short paragraphs according to a set of criteria — to define the meaning, state the importance, and say which readings the term or phrase refers to, for example, technical terminology such as "heteroglossic spatiality," referring to multiple communities with a common Oceanian space; a translation from Bislama or other pidgin English languages; the names of key voyaging craft, from the *Hokule'a* to the *Discovery*; or the evocation of fundamental concepts in Polynesian societies, such as the different expressions of kapu/tapu/tabu/taboo.[13]

You can also reference imposed categories such as "the Native Mother," created by colonial government to represent a hapless figure in need of imperial child-rearing education; or legendary cargo cult figures like John Frum. You could cite brief passages from poets like Grace Molisa or assumptions about female sexuality related by the anthropologist Margaret Mead. Questions of labor can be evoked by asking what students understand about the indentured servitude of Blackbirding, or the role of sea cucumbers, sandalwood, or seal furs in commodity chains involving Europeans, Islanders, and Asians.

Definitely do also incorporate visual exercises. Present images for interpretation and understanding, offering guidance for drawing out meaning, importance, and connections to texts or issues in the course. For example, illustrations could help students grasp the role of the Muslim Chinese Admiral Zheng He and his Treasure Fleet. Equally, prints representing encounters on the beach between European explorers and indigenous Islanders can be analyzed for the dynamics of curiosity, mistrust, and mutual political motives. Presenting works of art from multiple cultures — whether temple sculptures and reliefs from Java, rock paintings by Australian Aborigines, Kabuki masks from Japan, or carvings from the Sepik River Valley in New Guinea — can force students not only to broaden their aesthetic preferences, but to understand local materials, styles, cultural expressions, and social and political constraints.

Pictures of Christian missionaries may be less interesting than those of native agents, that is, indigenous Islanders spreading the gospel in their own communities, with their complex motivations. Familiar military images from the Opium Wars or the Battle of Iwo Jima can be paired with less familiar pictures of local scouts and Pacific battalions, or images of women and children in prison camps. More contemporary images of protest movements, sovereignty struggles, and environmental activism (think Greenpeace), land and sea rights (especially in Hawai'i and New Zealand), or nuclear testing (Tahiti and Moorea) present striking legacies with deep and debated meanings.

For essays, broadly ranging and thematic questions work well, particularly those that question the assumptions of the field itself, or that ask students not only to relate material about the subjects at hand, but to interrogate the definition of terms. Consider large questions, for example: A generation ago historians of the Pacific would have started their story with European exploration. How has the history we have been learning in class so far been different, and how can this difference be explained? What are some new approaches, actors, and events, and what insights do we gain from them?

CHAPTER TEN

Key vocabularies can be question topics, for example: How are navigation and diaspora critical concepts in Pacific history? Are these terms or experiences unique to defining Pacific peoples? Why have scholars spent so much time trying to re-create ancient voyages or studying maritime histories? Or, for the engagement of different narratives into a dialectic of power: Encounters between Asians, Islanders, and Europeans have long been sources of debate in global history. How would you describe and situate the meaning of encounters in the Pacific? Choose examples of the expectations of different participants, short- and long-term outcomes, and the motivations and interests that may have shaped them.

Regarding some classic critical challenges, students can be asked: What is the meaning of imperialism in the Pacific context? Does it have specific characteristics when applied to island peoples? Give examples. Consider not only administrative and economic explanations, but also the anthropological role of culture (which you'll define) in the shaping both of colonial and anticolonial projects. What are some of the legacies of these projects?

To provide interdisciplinary context, and for students with interests in applied knowledge, questions about economic matters can be engaging: Since the nineteenth century, trade and business have arguably played increasingly dominant roles in shaping the experience of Pacific peoples and their societies. How would you characterize the effects of trade and commercial interests? Give examples. Are they related to other questions we have studied, such as empire or globalization? Give examples of the motivations, connections, intentions, and ramifications for our understanding of the Pacific world.

Certainly, few history surveys would fail to focus on one of the mainstays of historical thinking and writing: conflict. For example: What is the meaning and logic of the Pacific War? Is it the same as World War II in Europe? From multiple perspectives, can you suggest when the Pacific War began and ended (if it did)? Think about the dates and events around, for example, the German invasion of Poland and the Japanese invasion of Manchuria. For the Pacific War, what were its reasons, outcomes, and legacies? In what ways was the war part of a larger global conflict, and in what ways was it motivated by social and political struggles particular to island peoples? Give examples. What are the connections with such wide-ranging "postwar" phenomena as cargo cults and nuclear testing? Students with military training or background often find these issues compelling.

The most truly engaging way to work through Pacific history, however, manifests not so much in exams as in project-based learning: that is, students should be charged to come up with their own way of thinking through a Pacific issue and presenting it in a scholarly format—with the definition of "scholarly" widely reimagined.

A good approach here is to provide students with an archive of possible entry points into Pacific histories. They can be both popular and successful because they meet the students where they are and draw them in, often through lenses of popular culture (anime), personal identity practices (tattooing), food (culture and ethnic cuisine), professional issues (public health, global finance), or institutional representations (museums). A set of such entry points might include, in no particular order but according to thematic categories and then ideas and examples:

Pop culture (contemporary expressions and challenges), television (Hawai'i, fantasy islands, survivor reality shows), anime and manga renditions

Body cults (tattooing and piercing), cuisine (luau, mixed plate, Spam)

Pacific War (veterans and remembrances), trust territories (administration and Peace Corps)

Pacific Rim I (Asian and Spanish heritages), Pacific Rim II (legacies of the Americas, rising powers and Southeast Asia)

Pacific Century (economic development and business), film (documentaries and dramas)

Tourism (postcards and tours), cannibalism, headhunting (ethnology and popular imagery)

Science, biology, Darwinism (natural history and selection, fatal impacts), ecology, flora, and fauna (island ecologies)

Easter Island (mysteries and totems), navigation (theories of arrival, *Kon-Tiki*, *Hokule'a*)

Dance and music (didgeridoo, ukulele, rhythm), island-inspired fashion (muumuu, sarong, aloha shirt, bikini)

Medicine (tropical disease and treatment, traditional cures), sports (surfing, diving)

Christianity and religion (missionaries and cults)

National liberation movements (New Caledonia, Fiji)

Paradise (European and American literature), kinship relations, rites (family and individuality)

Literature and poetry (new voices, writing back), sexuality, power, liberation, prostitution (imaginaries and realities)

Gods and Europeans (Sahlins and Obeyeskere), nuclear testing (French colonialism)

The arts (Maori, Guinean, Gauguin, and others), society of abundance (unspoiled representations of elysian islands)

Colonialism (administration and ideology), kapu, tabu, mana (universes of belief)

The museum (representing cultures), games (traditional and educational)

Racial typing and anthropology (Polynesians, Melanesians, Micronesians), cargo cult (cultural collision)

Contemporary geopolitical struggles (China and its neighbors in the South China Sea, export economy competition, China, Japan, North Korea, the United States, and nuclear diplomacy)

The final project for the course should be designed to give students a chance to explore and develop class themes and problems by focusing on a subject of their own choice. The list is just to provide ideas; ideally, students will be developing — or have already had — particular interests they wish to investigate. Projects are therefore intended to analytically draw together much of what the student has learned in the class, by concentrating that broad knowledge around a particular, detailed study, but they need not use the academic essay format. A project may, for example, incorporate materials presented visually, musically, kinetically, or gastronomically, in class if desired.

A project could be presented in lecture form, as drama or performance, or as a demonstration involving live actors, video clips, slides, overhead transparencies, or music and other forms of multimedia. For example, a design for a Pacific museum might include descriptions and explanations within the context of a museum proposal itself, utilizing different types of electronic media, with plans for programs and enactments. A planned series of lectures explaining the Pacific to a target audience might consist of the lectures themselves, framed by an intellectual rationale. Projects involving the creation of books, games, or other media might pose intellectual and historical problems as part of their own narratives.

Students could refer to the objectives of the course as stated in the syllabus: "to investigate and understand migration and navigation, cross-cultural contacts, nation building, ethnic identities, biological and ecological crises, legacies of colonialism and tourism, and the meanings of the Pacific Rim and the Pacific Century." Students could think of paradise, savagery, indigenous culture, encounter, images, representations, imperialism, anthropology, Pacific war, and development in the nuclear age, to name but a few themes. A good project will show what has been learned during the term, and how broad and specific connections have been incorporated into original thinking. A mediocre project will simply describe some special interest, with no attempt to link it thematically to larger goals. Poor projects are simply summaries of book and internet information.

Explore the Digital World

All of the above projects can be situated in the study of documents, sources, diaries, and archives, all of which are the traditional materials of historians. Pacific histories are likewise significantly anchored in the examination of artifacts and objects, in part because of the domain's roots in archaeological and ethnological study. For students in the current generation, access to museums, research libraries, and special collections is not the only means available. Though access to original sources is highly desired—and field study even more so—the truth is that much of the reference base is accessible in the digital world.

Many institutions have organized digital references to research aids, resources, maps and charts, video collections, and teaching syllabi collected from all across the Pacific region. The University of Hawai'i has been particularly noteworthy in this regard, with subjects in many media ranging from broad surveys to specific historical periods and thematic issues dealing with culture, the arts, environment, or literature (https://hawaii.edu/cpis/research-and-publications/research-aids-resources/). These are obviously useful to teachers, yet also for students who are eager to see how history is interpreted and taught across a wide range of geographic locales and specialties. It is particularly useful to understand how instructors in North American institutions frame questions differently from, say, teachers in Fiji, New Zealand, or Australia.

A number of institutions also have digitized online collections for research. The best are museums, such as the Bishop Museum in Honolulu, with its excellent online references to objects it holds; the Pacific Manuscripts Bureau, which has created digital collections of microfilms, photographs, documents, and registers from around Oceania, particularly the northern Pacific; and the National Library of Australia, with its reading rooms and superb digitized collection of prints, maps, paintings, and documents spanning centuries. To relate Pacific history to global history, I have emphasized focusing on commodities, materials, and products. I can recommend the collaborative network called Global Commodities.[14]

Of course, digital also means interactive, and many island identity groups—particularly for peoples who are linked to Pacific histories as part of a global diaspora—proliferate on the internet and allow keeping up with current issues and old questions in detail, much in the same way that portals like Facebook and Twitter have become media of both mass and interpersonal communication. The social media realm is, needless to say, also crowded with sites and individuals dedicated to Pacific issues. Many scholarly collectives, such as the World History Association, also use Twitter to host forums dealing with specific Oceanian issues (#whapchat pacific).

Regarding contemporary issues and daily news feeds, Professor Tara Kabutaulaka particularly recommends:

1 The *Pacific Islands Report* (http://pidp.eastwestcenter.org/pireport). Daily news stories and extensive links to other sites and resources, as well as a searchable archive.
2 ABC Radio Australia, programs like *Pacific Beat*, *Pacific Review*, *Pacific Mornings*, and *Wantok* (https://www.abc.net.au/radio-australia/). These broadcasts and podcasts present interviews with Pacific Island leaders and other newsmakers in the Pacific.

For other, especially visual, sources, see also the digital collections of the University of Hawai'i library with archival, anthropological, photographic, cartographic, and other rich sources of primary documentation and records. (https://manoa.hawaii.edu/library/research/collections/digital-image-collection/explore-our-digital-collections/).

Feature films make for excellent discussions. I have for many years benefited greatly by being able to build discussions around Geoff Murphy's *Utu*, about the land and political struggles in nineteenth-century Aotearoa/New Zealand. The narrative concerns a Maori warrior, Te Wheke, a scout for the British who turns against his nominal confreres when his own family is slaughtered in a British colonial raid. The depictions are both dramatic and didactic: the questionable portrayal of ritual vengeance; the collaborator who becomes a rebel; the arrogant church parson who finds his beliefs contradicted by his own moral message; the sympathetic homesteaders who find themselves unable to understand the deeper process of history around them; the allegorical battle between two men who are able to kill others, but not each other.

This can be paired with another film about a Maori family, the renowned *Once Were Warriors* (see chapter 8), based on Alan Duff's acclaimed novel and directed by Lee Tamahori, which again plays out both drama and history lesson: a father who is brutally strong but spiritually weak; a mother who seeks to protect her family but is too accepting of her fate; sons who are drawn to finding their way through tradition and separation; a daughter who is fated to carry the beauty of a culture to a tragic conclusion. In both films, the characters can be understood to embody historical principles — past, present, future, struggle, acquiescence, identity, and deracination — in worlds of colonial legacies.

Films such as these are engaging counterparts to other representations that raise the salient and persistent question of the degree to which Pacific peoples can be represented. Early cinematic works such as F. W. Murnau's *Tabu* are exemplary of the paradisical vision of island peoples as children of nature, even within the framework of an imposed Romeo and Juliet tale. More recent imaginings such as *Tanna* also combine the ethnographic and the romantic, with similar interests in mind. Other classics in particular genres include, for example, on atomic testing in the Pacific Islands, both Dennis O'Rourke's *Half Life* and Robert Stone's *Radio Bikini*, which make trenchant use of U.S. government propaganda film sources. Vicente Diaz's *Sacred Vessels* is an early documentary about the important role of voyaging canoes in Islander cultures and histories. In the ethnographic realm, classics like O'Rourke's *Cannibal Tours* examine the ways that tourism both shapes and fails communities in the Sepik River Valley of Papua New Guinea.

For extraordinary filmed perspectives, engage with the collections of Pacific Islanders in Communications — a major distributor of film, video, and other materials. The critical point here is that this is not only a fine and constantly evolving fund of culture, history, politics, and lore about Pacific peoples, but a significant source of works created by Islanders, offering unique perspectives, notably Puhipau and Joan Lander's *Act of War: The Overthrow of the Hawaiian Nation*. Dramatic works include a Fijian girl's search for justice in *The Land Has Eyes* by Jeannette and Vilsoni Hereniko and Merata Mita, and Niki Caro's *Whale Rider*, in which twelve-year-old Pai must overcome resistance in her own family to become a community leader. And consider how many students may be familiar with popular culture entertainments like the Disney Studios' *Moana*, which also follows themes of ancestry, voyaging, and realizing one's own place within an Oceanian universe. The Public Television series *Family Ingredients* traces multiple cultures and Pacific locales from Hawai'i, Vietnam, California, and the Philippines through the locus of food and kinship connections.[15]

For a remarkably detailed catalog collection of references to documentaries and features, as well as links to distributors, see Moving Images of the Pacific Islands: A Guide to Films and Videos (http://www.hawaii.edu/oceanic/film/) and Moving Images of the Pacific Islands (dahi.manoa.hawaii.edu/mipi/index.php/Main). Other sites recommended by Pacific culture and film scholar Professor Alexander Mawyer include Pacific Film, Filmmakers and Film Criticism: Finding Films (https://guides.library.manoa.hawaii.edu/pacfilm) and South Seas Cinema (http://www.southseascinema.org).

For a stronger Asian focus, the electronic resources of the Association for Asian Studies are exemplary, particularly in terms of outreach to teachers (https://www.asian-studies.org). The Education about Asia archive has a rich and engrossing, searchable collection that features interviews, projects in experiential learning, online supplements, teaching resource essays, features, and digital references ranging over food cultures (soy sauce, rice), environmental resources (oceans, rivers, coastal lands), teaching materials from demographics to political briefs, family heritage and lineage studies, biographies, migrations, ancient and modern science, and multiple recommendations or chronicles on teaching global-comparative or Asia-focused Pacific histories.

Tools to employ graphic novels and popular media in teaching or cinema are featured—for example, Korean, Japanese, Chinese, and Indian films. Short pieces on contemporary pop music and video genres even include helpful hints and primers of their own: who to listen to or watch to be current.

Happily, Asia-focused Pacific resources are widely collected, and teachers can explore any number of excellent collections, most of which are designed to assist teachers and provide materials for lessons and for engaging with students. For images, illustrations, and interpretations, particularly organized around Japan and China, see the MIT Visualizing Cultures collection (https://ocw.mit.edu/ans7870/21f/21 f.027/home/index.html). Specifically targeted for teachers, Columbia University's Weatherhead East Asian Institute created Asia for Educators (http://afe.easia.columbia.edu/), which has not only lesson plans and primary sources, but very helpful timelines, thematic summaries of key elements in chronologies across multiple civilizations and cultures, and integrated databases that allow searching for keyword topics across resource types including films and videos, illustrations and slides, maps and atlases, online units, teacher's guides, and audio.

You can piece together elements that you find useful and interesting, or take guidance directly from the samples and benchmark teaching plans. To add arts and languages to your material, take a look at recommendations curated by faculty at ASIANetwork (http://www.asianetwork.org/resources/resources-for-teaching/).

Students can also think about how film is not a stand-alone medium, but is often integrated with other projects run by organizations around the world. A notable example is the global Okeanos Foundation for the Sea, which has sponsored the revival of traditional Oceanian sailing with a vaka moana (oceangoing sailing canoe) initiative, supporting the building of state-of-the-art yet traditional canoes, working with Islander communities to engage culture, tradition, history, and environmentally sustainable transportation practices. These networks are supported in turn by film projects detailing the resiliency of local cultures and the threats of climate change, overfishing, and ocean pollution as a means to create political awareness and launch advocacy campaigns.

Think about the Goals

The goal is to engage students themselves with the experience of history and historical production. Beyond teaching and testing, another salutary way to address the fashioning of history is by consciously engaging students to produce historical thinking in the genre of memoir. This way, students will effectively begin their studies, in certain regards, at the endpoint. That is, have them imagine how their own lives have fashioned who they are, not individually and narcissistically, but in terms of their embodiments of broader forces and the legacy of generations.

Many scholars have done this to powerful effect through memoirs or chronicles of their own life histories. While more senior historians write memoirs, most younger scholars can also explain the reasons for their interests in history, often drawing together the logic of personal narrative, family reflection, and academic knowledge. Though they are not looking back over long careers, they nonetheless can situate themselves in ways that bring together their own life stories along with how their lives and commitments have overlapped with and intersected multiple questions about identity and connectedness to the past in their own communities. For students, this can be a revelation and a way for them to realize that their own interests, commitments, and lived histories issue from the same engagements with knowledge seeking, genealogy, social justice, decolonization, or immigration that have informed what are now academic pursuits: ethnic studies, fieldwork around the world, and discussions that interweave poetry with research, scholarship, and personal storytelling.[16]

Thus the writer becomes the manifestation of the history being told, while not being the subject himself or herself. This provides a challenging and also elegant model of how Pacific histories might be taught and learned; the embodiment of ideas and experiences, the learning of differences, and an understanding of the past that profoundly manifests in the present. In my own teaching, part of the hope is to provide students with the classic foundations of all historical thinking, reading, and writing. Through this, the goals include a grasp of basic elements: students will have a solid grasp of key figures, cultures, events, and chronologies in Pacific history.

Further, students will develop an understanding of major themes in the historical analysis of Pacific history: migration and navigation of island peoples, cross-cultural contacts, social organization, ethnic diasporas, ecological and biological crises, integration in a global commercial economy, nation building, struggles for sovereignty and identity, legacies of colonialism, and tourism. In addition, I like to organize an investigation around just a couple of big ideas: the Pacific Century and the Pacific Way have gained a great deal of attention in the last few years. What do these terms mean applied not only to the present, but to the centuries-long history of the Pacific? Classes will range over many types of sources, considering not only political tracts and documents but tourist materials, film and literary representations, oral accounts, performances and artifacts, flora and fauna, as well as financial, scientific, and medical studies.

Above all, the point is not only for students to read and learn, but perhaps to engage with history as a way of launching themselves into a deep and complex world, built around their own travel, navigations, journeys, studies, engagements, and commitments. Historical practice maintains itself as an expression of living cultures and constantly relearned knowledge regarding ancestors, acknowledging challenges and struggles, building futures. Students may grasp this as a domain that is finally about memory and history, finding that their experience is open to historical time and space, even as boundaries are recognized, tying them to as grand a world as the Pacific.

—— *Notes* ——

Introduction

1. Vilsoni Hereniko and Rob Wilson, eds., *Inside Out: Literature, Cultural Politics, and Identity in the New Pacific* (Lanham, MD: Rowman and Littlefield, 1999); Stephanie Lawson, ed., *Europe and the Asia-Pacific: Culture, Identity, and Representations of Region* (New York: Routledge, 2003).
2. Lynn Hunt, Thomas R. Martin, Barbara H. Rosenwein, and Bonnie G. Smith, *The Making of the West: Peoples and Cultures*, 5th ed. (Boston: Bedford/St. Martin's, 2016); David Armitage and Michael J. Braddick, eds., *The British Atlantic World, 1500–1800* (London: Palgrave-Macmillan, 2002); Paul Gilroy, *The Black Atlantic: Modernity and Double Consciousness* (Cambridge, MA: Harvard University Press, 1993); Andre Gunder Frank, *Re-Orient: Global Economy in the Asian Age* (Berkeley: University of California Press, 1998).
3. Rainer Buschmann, *Oceans in World History* (New York: McGraw-Hill, 2006); Oskar Spate, *The Pacific since Magellan* (3 vols.; Canberra: Australian National University Press, 2010); Greg Dening, *Beach Crossings: Voyaging across Times, Cultures, and Self* (Philadelphia: University of Pennsylvania Press, 2004); Nicholas Thomas, *Islanders: The Pacific in the Age of Empire* (New Haven, CT: Yale University Press, 2010); John Gascoigne, *Encountering the Pacific in the Age of Enlightenment* (Cambridge: Cambridge University Press, 2014); David Armitage and Alison Bashford, *Pacific Histories: Ocean, Land, People* (London: Palgrave, 2014); Tracey Banivanua-Mar, *Decolonisation and the Pacific: Indigenous Globalisation and the Ends of Empire* (Cambridge: Cambridge University Press, 2016); Hereniko and Wilson, *Inside Out*.
4. Shane Barter and Michael Wiener, eds., *The Pacific Basin: An Introduction* (New York: Routledge, 2017); Dennis Flynn and Arturo Giraldez, eds., *Studies in Pacific History: Economics, Politics, Migration* (New York: Routledge, 2018).

One. Begin with the State of Our Knowledge

1. Patrick Vinton Kirch, *On the Road of the Winds: An Archaeological History of the Pacific Islands before European Contact* (Berkeley: University of California Press, 2002).
2. Lisa Matisoo-Smith and J. H. Robins, "Origins and Dispersals of Pacific Peoples: Evidence from mtDNA Phylogenies of the Pacific Rat," *Proceedings of the National Academy of Sciences of the United States of America* 101, no. 24 (2004): 9167.
3. Bernice Pauahi Bishop Museum, https://www.bishopmuseum.org/.
4. Herb Kawainui Kane, *Voyagers* (Captain Cook, HI: Kawainui Press, 1991).
5. Darrell T. Tryon, *Bislama: An Introduction to the National Language of Vanuatu* (Canberra: Pacific Linguistics, RSPAS, 1987); "Bislama," *I Love Vanuatu*, October 14, 2009, http://ilovevanuatu.blogspot.com/2009/10/bislama.html; I. C. Campbell, *A History of the Pacific Islands* (Berkeley: University of California Press, 1989), 14–17.

Two. Secure the Fundamentals

1. Ben Finney, *From Sea to Space: The MacMillian Brown Lectures* (Honolulu: University of Hawai'i Press, 1992).
2. David Lewis, *We the Navigators: The Ancient Art of Landfaring in the Pacific* (Honolulu: University of Hawai'i Press, 1994); Polynesian Voyaging Society, http://pvs.kcc.hawaii.edu; Thor Heyerdahl, *The Kon-Tiki Expedition: By Raft across the South Seas* (London: Allen and Unwin, 1948).
3. Kerry Howe, *Where the Waves Fall* (Honolulu: University of Hawai'i Press, 1984).
4. Bronislaw Malinowski, *Argonauts of the Western Pacific* (Long Grove, IL: Waveland, 2013; orig. pub. 1922).
5. Margaret Mead, *Coming of Age in Samoa: A Study of Adolescence and Sex in Primitive Societies* (New York: Penguin, 1943); Jared Diamond, *Collapse: How Societies Choose to Fail or Survive* (New York: Penguin, 2013).

Three. Underscore the Connections

1. Leonard Andaya, *Leaves of the Same Tree: Trade and Ethnicity in the Straits of Melaka* (Honolulu: University of Hawai'i Press, 2008).
2. Louise Levathes, *When China Ruled the Seas: The Treasure Fleet of the Dragon Throne, 1405–1433* (New York: Oxford University Press, 1996).
3. Michael Powles, ed., *China and the Pacific: The View from Oceania* (Wellington, NZ: Victoria University Press, 2016).

4 Thomas Suárez, *Early Mapping of the Pacific: The Epic Story of Seafarers, Adventurers, and Cartographers Who Mapped the Earth's Greatest Ocean* (North Clarendon, VT: Tuttle, 2013).
5 Jean Gelman Taylor, *Indonesia: Peoples and Histories* (New Haven, CT: Yale University Press, 2004).
6 Rainer Buschmann, *Navigating the Spanish Lake: The Pacific in the Iberian World, 1521–1898* (Honolulu: University of Hawai'i Press, 2014).
7 Charles E. Nowell, *Magellan's Voyage around the World: Three Contemporary Accounts [by] Antonio Pigafetta, Maximilian of Transylvania [and] Gaspar Correa* (Evanston, IL: Literary Licensing, 2012; orig. pub. 1962).
8 Ikuo Higashibaba, *Christianity in Early Modern Japan: Kirishitan Belief and Practice* (Leiden: Leiden University Press, 2001); Joseph Francis Moran, *The Japanese and the Jesuits: Alessandro Valignano in Sixteenth-Century Japan* (London: Routledge, 1993).
9 Dian Murray, *Pirates of the South China Coast, 1790–1810* (Stanford, CA: Stanford University Press, 1987); Tonio Andrade, *How Taiwan Became Chinese: Dutch, Spanish, and Han Colonization in the Seventeenth Century* (New York: Columbia University Press, 2008).

Four. Review Disputed Legacies and Arguments

1 Dennis O. Flynn and Arturo Giraldez, "Born with a 'Silver Spoon': The Origin of World Trade in 1571," *Journal of World History* 6 (fall 1995): 201–21; Meha Priyadarshini, *Chinese Porcelain in Colonial Mexico: The Material Worlds of an Early Modern Trade* (London: Palgrave, 2018).
2 Tatiana Seijas, *Asian Slaves in Colonial Mexico: From Chinos to Indians* (Cambridge: Cambridge University Press, 2015).
3 John Gascoigne, *Encountering the Pacific in the Age of Enlightenment* (Cambridge: Cambridge University Press, 2014).
4 Leslie Stevenson, David L. Haberman, Peter Matthews Wright, and Charlotte Witt, *Thirteen Theories of Human Nature* (Oxford: Oxford University Press, 2017).
5 Horace Miner, "Body Ritual among the Nacirema" (New York: Irvington Reprint Series, 1993).
6 I. C. Campbell, *"Gone Native" in Polynesia: Captivity Narratives and Experiences from the South Pacific* (Westport, CT: Praeger, 1998).
7 David Chappell, *Double Ghosts: Oceanian Voyagers on Euroamerican Ships* (London: Routledge, 1997).
8 Marshall Sahlins, *How "Natives" Think: About Captain Cook, for Example*

(Chicago: University of Chicago Press, 1996); Gananath Obeyesekere, *The Apotheosis of Captain Cook: European Mythmaking in the Pacific* (Princeton, NJ: Princeton University Press, 1992).

9 George S. Kanahele, *Ku Kanak: Stand Tall; A Search for Hawaiian Values* (Honolulu: University of Hawai'i Press, 1992).

10 Ryan Jones, *Empire of Extinction: Russians and the North Pacific's Strange Beasts of the Sea, 1741–1867* (New York: Oxford University Press, 2017).

11 John Dunmore, *Vision and Realities: France in the Pacific, 1695–1995* (New York: Heritage, 1997).

12 Adrienne Kaeppler, "Artificial Curiosities," in *An Exposition of Native Manufacturers Collected on the Three Pacific Voyages of Captain James Cook, R.N.* (Honolulu: Bishop Museum Press, 1978); James Delbourgh, *Collecting the World: Hans Sloane and the Origins of the British Museum* (Cambridge, MA: Harvard University Press, 2017).

13 David Harvey, *The French Enlightenment and Its Others: The Mandarin, the Savage, and the Invention of the Human Sciences* (New York: Palgrave Macmillan, 2012).

14 Bronwen Douglass, *Science, Voyages, and Encounters in Oceania, 1511–1850* (London: Palgrave, 2014).

15 Greg Dening, *Mr. Bligh's Bad Language: Passion, Power, and Theater on the Bounty* (Cambridge: Cambridge University Press, 1992).

16 Doug Munno and Andrew Thornley, eds., *The Covenant Makers: Islander Missionaries in the Pacific* (Suva, Fiji: Pacific Theological College, 1996). For a first-person account, see Ron and Marjorie Crocombe, *Works of Ta'unga* (Honolulu: University of Hawai'i Press, 1968).

Five. Imperialism as a Teaching Tool

1 Nicholas Thomas, *Islanders: The Pacific in the Age of Empire* (New Haven, CT: Yale University Press, 2012).

2 Frederic W. Howay, ed., *Voyages of the Columbia to the Northwest Coast, 1787–1790 and 1790–1793* (Portland: Oregon Historical Society Press, 1990).

3 Joan Druett, ed., *She Was a Sister Sailor: The Whaling Journals of Mary Brewster, 1848–1851* (Mystic, CT: Mystic Seaport Museum, 1992).

4 Paul Van Dyke, *The Canton Trade: Life and Enterprise on the China Coast, 1700–1845* (Hong Kong: Hong Kong University Press, 2005).

5 Stephen Nichols, ed., *Convict Workers: Reinterpreting Australia's Past* (Cambridge: Cambridge University Press, 1998); Stuart MacIntyre, Anna Clark, and Anthony Mason, *The History Wars* (Melbourne: Melbourne University Press,

2004); Mark McKenna, *Looking for Blackfella's Point: An Australian History of Place* (Sydney: University of New South Wales Press, 2002).
6 Miranda Johnson, *The Land Is Our History: Indigeneity, Law, and the Settler State* (Oxford: Oxford University Press, 2016).
7 James Belich, *The New Zealand Wars and the Victorian Interpretation of Racial Conflict* (Auckland: Auckland University Press, 1986).
8 Geoff Murphy, dir., *Utu* (New Zealand Film Commission, 1983), with Anzac Wallace and Bruno Lawrence.
9 Haunani-Kay Trask, *From a Native Daughter: Colonialism and Sovereignty in Hawai'i*, rev. ed. (Honolulu: University of Hawai'i Press, 1999).
10 Joshua Reid, *The Sea Is My Country: The Maritime World of the Makahs* (New Haven, CT: Yale University Press, 2015).
11 Pietra Rivoli, *The Travels of a T-Shirt in the Global Economy: An Economist Examines the Markets, Power, and Politics of World Trade* (New York: Wiley, 2005).
12 Ryan Jones, "Running into Whales: The History of the North Pacific from below the Waves," *American Historical Review* 118, no 2 (2013): 349–77.
13 Gregory Cushman, *Guano and the Opening of the Pacific World: A Global Ecological History* (Cambridge: Cambridge University Press, 2013).
14 Julia Lovell, *The Opium War: Drugs, Dreams and the Making of China* (London: Picador, 2011); Yangwen Zheng, *The Social Life of Opium in China* (Cambridge: Cambridge University Press, 2005).
15 Wolfgang Schivelbusch, *Tastes of Paradise: A Social History of Spices, Stimulants, and Intoxicants* (New York: Vintage, 1993); Woodruff D. Smith, "From Coffeehouse to Parlour: The Consumption of Coffee, Tea and Sugar in North-Western Europe in the Seventeenth and Eighteenth Centuries," in *Consuming Habits: Global and Historical Perspectives on How Cultures Define Drugs*, 2nd ed., ed. Jordan Goodman, Paul E. Lovejoy, and Andrew Sherratt (London: Routledge, 2007), 142–57; Global Commodities: Trade, Exploration and Cultural Exchange, http://www.globalcommodities.amdigital.co.uk/Introduction/NatureAndScope.
16 Frances Steel, *Oceania under Steam: Sea Transport and the Cultures of Colonialism, c. 1870–1914* (Manchester: Manchester University Press, 2011).
17 Marilyn Lake and Henry Reynolds, *Drawing the Global Colour Line: White Men's Countries and the Question of Racial Equality* (Melbourne: Melbourne University Press, 2008).
18 Tracey Banivanua-Mar, *Violence and Colonial Dialogue: The Australian-Pacific Indentured Labor Trade* (Honolulu: University of Hawai'i Press, 1997); Ron Takaki, *Pau Hana: Plantation Life and Labor in Hawai'i* (Honolulu: Univer-

sity of Hawaiʻi Press, 1983); Evelyn Hu-Dehart, *Across the Pacific: Asian Americans and Globalization* (Philadelphia: Temple University Press, 2003).
19 Gerald Horne, *The White Pacific: U.S. Imperialism and Black Slavery in the South Seas after the Civil War* (Honolulu: University of Hawaiʻi Press, 2007).
20 Mae Ngai, *The Lucky Ones: One Family and the Extraordinary Invention of Chinese America* (Princeton, NJ: Princeton University Press, 2012); Mae Ngai, *Impossible Subjects: Illegal Aliens and the Making of Modern America* (Princeton, NJ: Princeton University Press, 2004); Brij Lal, "Girmit, History, Memory," in *Bittersweet: The Indo-Fijian Experience*, ed. Brij Lal (Canberra: Pandanus Press, 2004), 1–24; Gary Okihiro, *Island World: A History of Hawaiʻi and the United States* (Berkeley: University of California Press, 2008); Takaki, *Pau Hana*; Hu-Dehart, *Across the Pacific*.
21 Eveline Durr and Philipp Schorch, eds., *Transpacific Americas: Encounters and Engagements between the Americas and the South Pacific* (New York: Routledge, 2015).
22 David Chang, *The World and All the Things upon It: Native Hawaiian Geographies of Exploration* (Minneapolis: University of Minnesota Press, 2016).
23 Durr and Schorch, *Transpacific Americas*.

Six. Anthropology and Ethnology as Teaching Tools

1 Bronislaw Malinowski, *Argonauts of the Western Pacific* (Long Grove, IL: Waveland, 2013; orig. pub. London, 1922); also Bronislaw Malinowski, *The Sexual Life of Savages in North-Western Melanesia* (Hartford, CT: Martino Fine Books, 2015; orig. pub. 1929); Margaret Mead, *Coming of Age in Samoa: A Study of Adolescence and Sex in Primitive Societies* (New York: Penguin, 1943).
2 Joost Coté and Gunawan Mohamad, eds., *On Feminism and Nationalism: Kartini's Letters to Stella Zeehandelaar, 1889–1903* (Melbourne: Monash University, 2005).
3 Totaram Sanadhya, *My Twenty-One Years in the Fiji Islands* (Suva, Fiji: Fiji Museum, 1991).
4 Benedict Anderson, *Imagined Communities: Reflections on the Origins and Spread of Nationalism* (London: Verso, 1983); Jonathan Spence, *The Search for Modern China* (New York: Norton, 1990); Michael Francis Laffan, *Islamic Nationhood and Colonial Indonesia: The Umma below the Winds* (Nashville, TN: Abingdon, 2003).

Seven. Conflict as a Teaching Tool

1. Don Richter, *Where the Sun Stood Still: The Untold Story of Sir Jacob Vouza and the Guadalcanal Campaign* (London: Toucan, 1992).
2. Geoff White and Lamont Lindstrom, *The Pacific Theater: Island Representations of World War II* (Honolulu: University of Hawai'i Press, 1989).
3. Ian Buruma, *The Wages of Guilt: Memories of War in Germany and Japan* (New York: New York Review Books, 2015).
4. Roger Thompson, *The Pacific Basin since 1945* (Oklahoma City, OK: Harlow, 2001).
5. Roland Spector, *In the Ruins of Empire: The Japanese Surrender and the Battle for Postwar Asia* (New York: Random House, 2001).
6. Tracey Banivanua-Mar, *Decolonisation and the Pacific: Indigenous Globalisation and the Ends of Empire* (Cambridge: Cambridge University Press, 2016).
7. Anna Lowenhaupt Tsing, *In the Realm of the Diamond Queen: Marginality in an Out-of-the-Way Place* (Princeton, NJ: Princeton University Press, 1993); David Gegeo, "Indigenous Knowledge and Empowerment: Rural Development Examined from Within," *Contemporary Pacific* 10, no. 2 (1998): 289–315.
8. Films: Robert Stone, dir., *Radio Bikini* (1988); Dennis O'Rourke, dir., *Half Life: A Parable for the Nuclear Age* (1985). See the excellent analysis contrasting nuclear testing and paradise images in Teresia Teaiwa, "Bikinis and Other S/Pacific N/Oceans," *Contemporary Pacific* 6, no. 1 (spring 1994): 87–109.
9. Jane Dibblin: *Day of Two Suns: U.S. Nuclear Testing and the Pacific Islanders* (New York: New Amsterdam, 1988); Barbara Rose Johnston and Holly Barker, *Consequential Damages of Nuclear War: The Rongelap Report* (New York: Routledge, 2008); Zohl de Ishtar, ed., *Pacific Women Speak Out for Independence and Denuclearisation* (Christchurch: Pacific Connections, 1998).
10. David Doulman, *Tuna Issues and Perspectives in the Pacific Islands Region* (Honolulu: East-West Center, 1987); Micah Muscolino, *Fishing Wars and Environmental Change in Late Imperial and Modern China* (Cambridge, MA: Harvard University Press, 2009).
11. Moses Havini and Vikki John, "Mining, Self-Determination, and Bougainville," in *Moving Mountains: Communities Confront Mining and Globalization*, ed. Geoffrey Russell Evans, James Goodman, and Nina Lansbury (London: Zed, 2001), chapter 8.

Eight. Identity as a Teaching Tool

1. Monina Allarey Mercado, ed., *People Power: The Philippine Revolution of 1986; An Eyewitness History* (Manila: James B. Reuter, S. J. Foundation, 1986).

2 Grace Mera Molisa, *Colonised People: Poems by Grace Mera Molisa* (Port Vila, Vanuatu: Blackstone, 1987); Margaret Jolly, *Women of the Place: Kastom, Colonialism and Gender in Vanuatu* (London: Harwood, 1994).
3 Alan Duff, *Once Were Warriors* (New York: Vintage, 1990).
4 Jeremy A. Murray and Kathleen M. Nadeau, *Pop Culture in Asia and Oceania* (Santa Barbara, CA: ABC-CLIO, 2016); Gabriel Solis, "The Black Pacific: Music and Racialization in Papua New Guinea and Australia," *Critical Sociology* 41, no. 2 (March 2014): 297–312.
5 Doris Pilkington, *Follow the Rabbit-Proof Fence* (Brisbane: University of Queensland Press, 1996).
6 Yoshiaki Yoshimi, *Comfort Women: Sexual Slavery in the Japanese Military during World War II* (New York: Columbia University Press, 1995); Iris Chang, *The Rape of Nanjing: The Forgotten Holocaust of World War II* (New York: Basic Books, 1998); John Mason, *The Pacific War Remembered: An Oral History* (Annapolis, MD: Naval Institute Press, 1986).
7 Hiroo Onoda, *No Surrender: My Thirty-Year War* (Tokyo: Kodansha, 1974).
8 Noenoe Silva, *Aloha Betrayed: Native Hawaiian Resistance to American Colonialism* (Durham, NC: Duke University Press, 2004).
9 Epeli Hau'ofa, "Our Sea of Islands," in *We Are the Ocean: Selected Works* (Honolulu: University of Hawai'i Press, 2008), 27–40.

Nine. Distinguish Representations and Realities

1 Lamont Lindstrom, *Cargo Cult: Strange Stories of Desire from Melanesia and Beyond* (Honolulu: University of Hawai'i Press, 1993).
2 Robin Helmey, *Invented Eden: The Elusive, Disputed History of the Tasaday* (Lincoln: University of Nebraska Press, 2006).
3 Valerie L. Smith, *Hosts and Guests: The Anthropology of Tourism* (Philadelphia: University of Pennsylvania Press, 1989); Peter M. Burns and Marina Novelli, *Tourism and Politics: Global Frameworks and Local Realities* (New York: Routledge, 2007).
4 Andrew Ross, "Cultural Preservation in the Polynesia of the Latter-Day Saints," in *The Chicago Gangster Theory of Life: Nature's Debt to Society* (New York: Verso, 1994), 21–98; Haunani-Kay Trask, "'Lovely Hula Hands': Corporate Tourism and the Prostitution of Hawaiian Culture," in *From a Native Daughter: Colonialism and Sovereignty in Hawai'i*, rev. ed. (Honolulu: University of Hawai'i Press, 1999), 136–48.
5 Mary Terrell Cargill and Jade Ngoc Quang Huynh, *Voices of the Vietnamese Boat People: Nineteen Narratives of Escape and Survival* (Jefferson, NC:

McFarland, 2000); "A True Story," June 1999, Boatpeople.org, http://www.boatpeople.org/a_true_story.htm.

6 Aihwa Ong, *Spirits of Resistance and Capitalist Discipline: Factory Women in Malaysia* (Albany: State University of New York Press, 1987); Toon van Meijl, "Beyond Economics: Transnational Labour Migration in Asia and the Pacific," *IIAS Newsletter*, no. 43 (spring 2007).

7 Peter Lehr, ed., *Violence at Sea: Piracy in the Age of Global Terrorism* (New York: Routledge, 2008).

Ten. See the Process of Enacting Knowledge

1 Joseph Aldy and Robert Stavins, eds., *Architectures for Agreement: Addressing Global Climate Change in the Post-Kyoto World* (Cambridge: Cambridge University Press, 2007).

2 Paul D'Arcy, "Oceania: The Environmental History of One-Third of the Globe," in *A Companion to Global Environmental History*, ed. J. R. McNeill and Erin Steward Maudlin (Chichester, UK: John Wiley, 2012), 196–221; Ryan Tucker Jones, "The Environment," in *Pacific Histories: Ocean, Land, People*, ed. David Armitage and Alison Bashford (London: Palgrave, 2014), 121–42.

3 Mark Borthwick, *Pacific Century: The Emergence of Modern Pacific Asia* (New York: Routledge, 2018); Frank Gibney, *The Pacific Century: America and Asia in a Changing World* (New York: Scribner's, 1992); James W. Morley, ed., *Driven by Growth: Political Change in the Asia-Pacific Region* (New York: Routledge, 1999).

4 Robert Fitzgerald and Chris Rowley, eds., *Multinational Companies from Japan* (New York: Routledge, 2016); Ezra F. Vogel, *The Four Little Dragons: The Spread of Industrialization in East Asia* (Cambridge, MA: Harvard University Press, 1991).

5 Chris Berry, Nicola Liscutin, and Jonathan D. Mackintosh, eds., *Cultural Studies and Cultural Industries in Northeast Asia: What a Difference a Region Makes* (Hong Kong: Hong Kong University Press, 2009).

6 Ademola A. Adenle, E. Jane Morris, and Denis J. Murphy, eds., *Genetically Modified Organisms in Developing Countries: Risk Analysis and Governance* (Cambridge: Cambridge University Press, 2017); Vandana Shiva, *Stolen Harvest: The Hijacking of the Global Food Supply* (Lexington: University Press of Kentucky, 2016).

7 Terence Wesley-Smith and Edgar A. Porter, eds., *China in Oceania: Reshaping the Pacific?* (New York: Berghahn, 2010); Wang Gungwu, *Renewal: The Chinese State and the New Global History* (Hong Kong: Chinese University Press, 2013).

8 Paul D'Arcy, "The Chinese Pacifics: A Brief Historical Review," *Journal of Pacific History* 49, no. 4 (2014): 396–420.
9 Elazar Barkan, *The Guilt of Nations: Restitution and Negotiating Historical Injustices* (New York: Norton, 2000); Jeanette Marie Mageo, *Cultural Memory: Reconfiguring History and Identity in the Postcolonial Pacific* (Honolulu: University of Hawai'i Press, 2001).
10 Elizabeth De Loughrey, *Routes and Roots: Navigating Caribbean and Pacific Island Literatures* (Honolulu: University of Hawai'i Press, 2007); Brian Russell Roberts and Michelle Ann Stephens, *Archipelagic American Studies* (Durham, NC: Duke University Press, 2017).
11 Susanne Berthier-Foglar, Sheila Collingwood-Whittick, and Sandrine Tolazzi, eds., *Biomapping Indigenous Peoples: Towards an Understanding of the Issues* (Amsterdam: Rodopi, 2012).
12 J. Kehaulani Kauanui, *Hawaiian Blood: Colonialism and the Politics of Sovereignty and Indigeneity* (Durham, NC: Duke University Press, 2008); Kim Tall Bear, *Native American DNA: Tribal Belonging and the False Promise of Genetic Science* (Minneapolis: University of Minnesota Press, 2013).
13 Arif Dirlik and Rob Wilson, eds., *Asia/Pacific as Space of Cultural Production* (Durham, NC: Duke University Press, 1995).
14 "Nature and Scope," Global Commodities: Trade, Exploration and Cultural Exchange, accessed August 26, 2019, http://www.globalcommodities.amdigital.co.uk/Introduction/NatureAndScope.
15 For films and media, see Pacific Islanders in Communication, https://www.piccom.org/.
16 Haunani-Kay Trask, *From a Native Daughter: Colonialism and Sovereignty in Hawai'i*, rev. ed. (Honolulu: University of Hawai'i Press, 1999); Linda Tuhiwai Smith, *Decolonizing Methodologies: Research and Indigenous Peoples* (London: Zed, 2012); Brij Lal, *Mr. Tulsi's Store: A Fijian Journey* (Canberra: Australian National University Press, 2013); Gary Y. Okihiro, *The Boundless Sea: Self and History* (Oakland: University of California Press, 2019); and the graphic novel by Thi Bui, *The Best We Could Do: An Illustrated Memoir* (New York: Harry Abrams, 2017).

———— *Selected Bibliography* ————

Andaya, Barbara. "Oceans Unbounded: Transversing Asia across 'Area Studies.'" *Journal of Asian Studies* 65, no. 4 (November 2006): 669–90.
Andaya, Leonard. *Leaves of the Same Tree: Trade and Ethnicity in the Straits of Melaka*. Honolulu: University of Hawai'i Press, 1994.
Anderson, Benedict. *Imagined Communities: Reflections on the Origin and Spread of Nationalism*. London: Verso, 1983.
Andrade, Tonio. *How Taiwan Became Chinese: Dutch, Spanish, and Han Colonization in the Seventeenth Century*. New York: Columbia University Press, 2008.
Antony, Robert. *Like Froth Floating on the Sea: The World of Pirates and Seafarers in Late Imperial South China*. Guangzhou: China Research Monograph, 2003.
Armitage, David, and Alison Bashford. *Pacific Histories: Ocean, Land, People*. London: Palgrave, 2014.
Banivanua-Mar, Tracey. *Decolonisation and the Pacific: Indigenous Globalisation and the Ends of Empire*. Cambridge: Cambridge University Press, 2016.
Barrera-Osorio, Antonio. *Experiencing Nature: The Spanish American Empire and the Early Scientific Revolution*. Austin: University of Texas Press, 2006.
Barter, Shane, and Michael Wiener, eds. *The Pacific Basin: An Introduction*. New York: Routledge, 2017.
Belich, James. *Making People: A History of the New Zealanders from Polynesian Settlement to the End of the Nineteenth Century*. Honolulu: University of Hawai'i Press, 2002.
Berthier-Foglar, Susanne, Sheila Collingwood-Whittick, and Sandrine Tolazzi, eds. *Biomapping Indigenous Peoples: Towards an Understanding of the Issues*. Amsterdam: Rodopi, 2012.
Borofsky, Robert, ed. *Remembrance of Pacific Pasts*. Honolulu: University of Hawai'i Press, 2000.
Borthwick, Mark. *Pacific Century: The Emergence of Modern Pacific Asia*. Boulder, CO: Westview, 2007.

Bose, Sugata. *A Hundred Horizons: The Indian Ocean in the Age of Global Empire.* Cambridge, MA: Harvard University Press, 2006.

Burns, Peter M., and Marina Novelli. *Tourism and Politics: Global Frameworks and Local Realities.* New York: Routledge, 2007.

Buschmann, Rainer F. *Iberian Visions of the Pacific Ocean, 1507–1899.* London: Palgrave, 2014.

Cargill, Mary Terrell, and Jade Ngoc Quang Huynh. *Voices of the Vietnamese Boat People: Nineteen Narratives of Escape and Survival.* Jefferson, NC: McFarland, 2000.

Chang, David. *The World and All the Things upon It: Native Hawaiian Geographies of Exploration.* Minneapolis: University of Minnesota Press, 2016.

Chappell, David. *Double Ghosts: Oceanian Voyagers on Euroamerican Ships.* London: Routledge, 1997.

Chaudhuri, K. N. *Asia before Europe: Economy and Civilization of the Indian Ocean from the Rise of Islam to 1750.* Cambridge: Cambridge University Press, 1991.

Cushman, Gregory. *Guano and the Opening of the Pacific World: A Global Ecological History.* Cambridge: Cambridge University Press, 2013.

D'Arcy, Paul. *The People of the Sea: Environment, Identity, and History in Oceania.* Honolulu: University of Hawai'i Press, 2006.

Dening, Greg. *Beach Crossings: Voyaging across Times, Cultures, and Self.* Philadelphia: University of Pennsylvania Press, 2004.

Denoon, Donald, Malama Meleisea, Stewart Firth, Jocelyn Linnekin, and Karen Nero, eds. *The Cambridge History of the Pacific Islanders.* Cambridge: Cambridge University Press, 1997.

Diamond, Jared. *Guns, Germs, and Steel: The Fates of Human Societies.* New York: Norton, 1997.

Douglas, Bronwen. *Science, Voyages, and Encounters in Oceania, 1511–1850.* London: Palgrave, 2014.

Dower, John. *War without Mercy: Race and Power in the Pacific War.* New York: Pantheon, 1987.

Dudden, Arthur Power, ed. *American Empire in the Pacific: From Trade to Strategic Balance, 1700–1922.* Vol. 9 of *The Pacific World: Lands, Peoples and History of the Pacific, 1500–1900.* New York: Routledge, 1992.

Duff, Alan. *Once Were Warriors.* New York: Vintage, 1990.

Durr, Eveline, and Philipp Schorch, eds. *Transpacific Americas: Encounters and Engagements between the Americas and the South Pacific.* New York: Routledge, 2015.

Finn, Richard. *Nature's Chemicals: The Natural Products That Shaped Our World.* New York: Oxford University Press, 2010.

Finney, Ben. *Voyage of Rediscovery: A Cultural Odyssey through Polynesia*. Berkeley: University of California Press, 1994.
Flynn, Dennis O., and Arturo Giraldez, eds. *The Pacific World: Lands, Peoples and History of the Pacific, 1500–1900*. 17 vols. London: Routledge, 2009.
Fogel, Joshua, ed. *The Nanjing Massacre: History and Historiography*. Berkeley: University of California Press, 2000.
Frank, Andre Gunder. *Re-Orient: Global Economy in the Asian Age*. Berkeley: University of California Press, 1998.
Freeman, Donald. *The Pacific*. London: Routledge, 2010.
Fujitani, Tak, Geoff White, and Lisa Yoneyama, eds. *Perilous Memories: The Asia-Pacific War(s)*. Durham, NC: Duke University Press, 2001.
Gascoigne, John. *Encountering the Pacific in the Age of Enlightenment*. Cambridge: Cambridge University Press, 2014.
Gordon, Andrew, ed. *Postwar Japan as History*. Berkeley: University of California Press, 1993.
Hauʻofa, Epeli. "Our Sea of Islands." In *We Are the Ocean: Selected Works*, 27–40. Honolulu: University of Hawaiʻi Press, 2008.
Hereniko, Vilsoni, and Rob Wilson, eds. *Inside Out: Literature, Cultural Politics, and Identity in the New Pacific*. New York: Rowman and Littlefield, 1999.
Horne, Gerald. *The White Pacific: U.S. Imperialism and Black Slavery in the South Seas after the Civil War*. Honolulu: University of Hawaiʻi Press, 2007.
Hourani, George F. *Arab Seafaring in the Indian Ocean in Ancient and Medieval Times*. Princeton, NJ: Princeton University Press, 1951.
Howe, Kerry R. *Vaka Moana, Voyages of the Ancestors: The Discovery and Settlement of the Pacific*. Honolulu: University of Hawaiʻi Press, 2007.
Igler, David. *The Great Ocean: Pacific Worlds from Captain Cook to the Gold Rush*. New York: Oxford University Press, 2013.
Johnston, Barbara Rose, and Holly Barker. *Consequential Damages of Nuclear War: The Rongelap Report*. New York: Routledge, 2008.
Jolly, Margaret. "Imagining Oceania: Indigenous and Foreign Representations of a Sea of Islands." *Contemporary Pacific* 19, no. 2 (2007): 508–45.
Jones, Ryan Tucker. "The Environment." In *Pacific Histories: Ocean, Land, People*, edited by David Armitage and Alison Bashford, 121–42. London: Palgrave, 2014.
Kauanui, J. Kehaulani. *Hawaiian Blood: Colonialism and the Politics of Sovereignty and Indigeneity*. Durham, NC: Duke University Press, 2008.
Kirch, Patrick Vinton. *On the Road of the Winds: An Archaeological History of the Pacific Islands before European Contact*. Berkeley: University of California Press, 2000.
Lake, Marilyn, and Henry Reynolds. *Drawing the Global Colour Line: White Men's

Countries and the Question of Racial Equality. Melbourne: Melbourne University Press, 2008.

Lehr, Peter, ed. *Violence at Sea: Piracy in the Age of Global Terrorism.* New York: Routledge, 2008.

Levathes, Louise. *When China Ruled the Seas: The Treasure Fleet of the Dragon Throne, 1405-33.* New York: Oxford University Press, 1994.

Lidin, Olof. *Tanegashima: The Arrival of Europeans in Japan.* Copenhagen: NIAS Press, 2002.

Lindstrom, Lamont. *Cargo Cult: Strange Stories of Desire from Melanesia and Beyond.* Honolulu: University of Hawai'i Press, 1993.

Liu, Lydia He. *The Clash of Empires: The Invention of China in Modern World Making.* Cambridge, MA: Harvard University Press, 2004.

Lovell, Julia. *The Opium War: Drugs, Dreams and the Making of China.* London: Picador, 2011.

Mageo, J. M., ed. *Cultural Memory: Reconfiguring History and Identity in the Postcolonial Pacific.* Honolulu: University of Hawai'i Press, 2001.

Matsuda, Matt K. *Empire of Love: Histories of France and the Pacific.* New York: Oxford University Press, 2003.

Matsuda, Matt K. *Pacific Worlds: A History of Seas, Peoples, and Cultures.* Cambridge: Cambridge University Press, 2012.

McKenna, Mark. *Looking for Blackfella's Point: An Australian History of Place.* Sydney: University of New South Wales Press, 2002.

Monaghan, Jay. *Chile, Peru, and the California Gold Rush of 1849.* Berkeley: University of California Press, 1973.

Murray, Jeremy A., and Kathleen M. Nadeau. *Pop Culture in Asia and Oceania.* Santa Barbara, CA: ABC-CLIO, 2016.

Ngai, Mae. *The Lucky Ones: One Family and the Extraordinary Invention of Chinese America.* Princeton, NJ: Princeton University Press, 2012.

Nicholas, Stephen, ed. *Convict Workers: Reinterpreting Australia's Past.* New York: Cambridge University Press, 1988.

Norindr, Panivong. *Phantasmatic Indochina: French Colonial Ideology in Architecture, Film, and Literature.* Durham, NC: Duke University Press, 1996.

Obeyesekere, Gananath. *The Apotheosis of Captain Cook: European Mythmaking in the Pacific.* Princeton, NJ: Princeton University Press, 1992.

Osorio, Jonathan K. *Dismembering Lahui: A History of the Hawaiian Nation to 1887.* Honolulu: University of Hawai'i Press, 2002.

Peattie, Mark. *Nan'yo: The Rise and Fall of the Japanese in Micronesia.* Honolulu: University of Hawai'i Press, 1988.

Punzalan Isaac, Allan. *American Tropics: Articulating Filipino America*. Minneapolis: University of Minnesota Press, 2006.
Reid, Joshua. *The Sea Is My Country: The Maritime World of the Makahs*. New Haven, CT: Yale University Press, 2015.
Robie, David. *Blood on Their Banner: Nationalist Struggles in the South Pacific*. London: Zed, 1989.
Rosenthal, Gregory. *Beyond Hawai'i: Native Labor in the Pacific World*. Berkeley: University of California Press, 2018.
Sahlins, Marshall. *Historical Metaphors and Mythical Realities*. Ann Arbor: University of Michigan Press, 1981.
Scott, James. *Weapons of the Weak*. New Haven, CT: Yale University Press, 1985.
Seijas, Tatiana. *Asian Slaves in Colonial Mexico: From Chinos to Indians*. Cambridge: Cambridge University Press, 2015.
Silva, Noenoe K. *Aloha Betrayed: Native Hawaiian Resistance to American Colonialism*. Durham, NC: Duke University Press, 2004.
Steel, Frances. *Oceania under Steam: Sea Transport and the Cultures of Colonialism, c. 1870–1914*. Manchester: Manchester University Press, 2011.
Stoler, Ann Laura. *Carnal Knowledge and Imperial Power: Race and the Intimate in Colonial Rule*. Berkeley: University of California Press, 2002.
Suárez, Thomas. *Early Mapping of the Pacific: The Epic Story of Seafarers, Adventurers, and Cartographers Who Mapped the Earth's Greatest Ocean*. Singapore: Periplus, 2004.
Tagliacozzo, Eric. *The Longest Journey: Southeast Asians and the Pilgrimage to Mecca*. New York: Oxford University Press, 2013.
Tagliacozzo, Eric, Helen F. Siu, and Peter C. Perdue, eds. *Asia Inside Out*. Vol. 1: *Changing Times*. Cambridge, MA: Harvard University Press, 2015.
Tagliacozzo, Eric, Helen F. Siu, and Peter C. Perdue, eds. *Asia Inside Out*. Vol. 2: *Connected Places*. Cambridge, MA: Harvard University Press, 2015.
Tagliacozzo, Eric, Helen F. Siu, and Peter C. Perdue, eds. *Asia Inside Out*. Vol. 3: *Itinerant People*. Cambridge, MA: Harvard University Press, 2019.
Takaki, Ron. *Pau Hana: Plantation Life and Labor in Hawaii*. Honolulu: University of Hawai'i Press, 1983.
Taylor, Jean Gelman. *Indonesia: Peoples and Histories*. New Haven, CT: Yale University Press, 2003.
Teaiwa, Teresia K. "Bikinis and Other S/Pacific N/Oceans." *Contemporary Pacific* 6, no. 1 (spring 1994): 87–109.
Thomas, Nicholas. *Entangled Objects: Exchange, Material Culture, and Colonialism in the Pacific*. Cambridge, MA: Harvard University Press, 1991.

Thomas, Nicholas. *Islanders: The Pacific in the Age of Empire*. New Haven, CT: Yale University Press, 2010.
Thompson, Roger. *The Pacific Basin since 1945*. London: Routledge, 2014.
Trask, Haunani-Kay. *From a Native Daughter: Colonialism and Sovereignty in Hawai'i*. Rev. ed. Honolulu: University of Hawai'i Press, 1999.
Tuhiwai Smith, Linda. *Decolonizing Methodologies: Research and Indigenous Peoples*. London: Zed, 2012.
Van Dyke, Paul A. *The Canton Trade: Life and Enterprise on the China Coast, 1700–1845*. Hong Kong: Hong Kong University Press, 2005.
Wesley-Smith, Terence, and Edgar A. Porter, eds. *China in Oceania: Reshaping the Pacific?* New York: Berghahn, 2010.
White, Geoffrey, and Lamont Lindstrom, eds. *Island Encounters: Black and White Memories of the Pacific War*. Washington, DC: Smithsonian, 1990.
White, Geoffrey, and Lamont Lindstrom. *The Pacific Theater: Island Representations of World War II*. Honolulu: University of Hawai'i Press, 1989.
Wilson, Rob, and Arif Dirlik, eds. "Introduction." In *Asia/Pacific as Space of Cultural Production*, 1–14. Durham, NC: Duke University Press, 1995.
Yoshimi, Yoshiaki. *Comfort Women: Sexual Slavery in the Japanese Military during World War II*. New York: Columbia University Press, 1995.

Index

Aboriginal peoples, 70, 71, 72, 108
Acapulco, port at, 43, 52
activism, 98–100, 133; women and, 92, 102, 104, 105–6
Act of War (movie), 75
Act of War: The Overthrow of the Hawaiian Nation (Puhipau and Lander), 140
actors, historical, 68–76; individuals, 68–69
administrative knowledge and practice, 125, 136
Ahutoru (island voyager), 56
aid donation politics, 126–27
alliances, political and international, 14
almanac approach, 14
American Board, 63
American Civil War, 83–84
Americas, 42–46, 85
Anderson, Benedict, 93
Anglophone perspectives, 11
anime and manga, 47, 124
anthropology and ethnology as teaching tools, 20, 89–94, 129–30, 135; idealized presentations, 91; material culture objects, 91; nationalist identities, 91–94; participant observation, 90; role of, 89–91

antinuclear movements, 102–3
antisettler and anticolonial struggles, 91–94, 136
Aotearoa/New Zealand, 72–73, 139
apology debates, 15
Apolosi Nawai (Fijian islander), 73–74
appropriation, cultural, 8
Aquino, Corazon, 105–6
Arabic influences, 34, 36
Arctic ice, melting of, 57
artifacts, 91; Lapita pottery, 20; moai statues of Easter Island/Rapa Nui, 20
artificial islands, 127
artists, 21–22
artworks, 133, 136
Asia, 12; imperialism, 74–75
Asia for Educators, 141–42
ASIANetwork, 142
Asian heritage, 33–38
Asian Pacific, 46–48
Asian Tigers, 85, 123
assemblage approach, 15, 19–21
assemblage model, 87
Association for Asian Studies, 141
assumptions about Pacific, 1–2, 4
Atlantic world, 13
Atlantis, 57

INDEX

atomic testing and fallout, 101–2
atomic warfare, 97, 101–3
Australasia, 9
Australia, 70–71; Aboriginal, Asian, and European communities, 72; Sorry Day, 15, 108
Australian National University, 126
Austronesian heritage, common, 25–26
Austronesian narrative, 126
authenticity, 91

Bali, 119–20
Banivanua-Mar, Tracey, 99
barangay communities, 36
Barter, Shane, 12
beachcomber figure, 55
Belt and Road Initiative (New Silk Road), 125–26
big ideas, 143–44
Big Man cultures, 29
biography, great-men, 45
biological and life sciences interest, 41–42, 61
biopolitics, 130–31
Bishop Museum (Honolulu), 21
Bislama language, 22, 132
"blackbirding," 83, 132
Black Pacific, 99–100
Black Panthers, 99
Bligh, William, 62
blood quantum debates, 131
"boat people," 118
body cults, 135
"Body Ritual among the Nacirema" (Miner), 55
borders, 30
Borneo, 72
Borobudur temple complex, 35
botanical interest, 41–42, 61, 62
Bougainville (island), 104

Bougainville, Louis Antoine de, 31, 54, 60
Bounty (ship), 62, 67
Braudel, Fernand, 33
Brewster, Mary, 69
Britain: Australia and, 70–71; Seven Years' War, 44, 45, 53
British historiography, 45
British navy, 40
Brooke, Rupert, 72
Brunei, 36
Buddha, 34–35
Buddhism, 39
Budi Utomo (group, Indonesia), 93
Buschmann, Rainer, 43
business interests, 41–42, 51–52; eighteenth-century globalization, 76–81; Enlightenment era, 59; local economies, 74

cabinet of curiosity collectibles, 60
Cakombau (Fijian chief), 73, 83
cannibalism, 57–58
Cannibal Tours (movie), 140
Canton, 70, 77
cargo cult, 113–15
castaways/shipwrecked sailors, 55–56
Catholic Church, 119; Jesuit priests, Portuguese, 47–48
cautionary tales, 32
Central Pacific, 54
Chang, David, 86
change, cultural, 55
Chappell, David, 56
Chiang Kai-shek, 98, 99
Chile, 87
Chilean immigrants, 88
China, 12; ancient, 34; Asian neighbors, 127; diversity, 127–28; economic leadership, 124, 125–28; empire and, 70; under Mao Zedong, 97–98; as

People's Republic, 126; Shang rulers (2000 BCE), 34
China Trade, 75
Chinese Treasure Fleets, 36–37, 125, 133
Christendom, medieval maps of, 39
Christians, 63–64, 114; in sixteenth-century Japan, 47–48
chronology, 4–6
Cipangu (Japan), 47
civilization, problematic aspects of, 58
class status, 81–82
climate change, 40, 57, 121–23
Clinton, Bill, 109
Cohong consortiums, 77
Cohong guild (Canton), 70
Cold War, 97, 98
collaboration, 46
colonialism, 136; antisettler and anticolonial struggles, 91–94; decolonization, 97–100; labor exploitation, 52; Native Mother trope, 132; settler, 68; unraveling of, 45. *See also* imperialism
"Colonised People" (Molisa), 107
Columbia University's Weatherhead East Asian Institute, 141–42
Columbus, Christopher, 46
comfort women (Japan), 128
Coming of Age in Samoa (Mead), 32, 90
commemorative sites, 15, 46, 109
commodities, 41, 76–81, 114, 132–33; Global Commodities network, 138; tourism as, 116–17
comparative cultures, 90
comparative traditions, 26
Comprador business agents, 76
conflict as teaching tool, 95–104; decolonization, 97–100; environmental issues and, 103–4; local politics, 100–101; Oceanian history as subset of colonial history, 98; postwar period, 98–99; testing and exam materials, 134–35; war and shaping of history, 95–97
constructedness of scholarly knowledge, 14, 22
contact zones, 33–49; Chinese Treasure Fleets, 36–38; Enlightenment era, 59–61; Europeans, 38–42; exploration, encounter, and discovery, 39; visual exercises, 133
Contemplacion, Flor, 118–19
contemporary politics, 119–20, 136
conventions, challenging, 14–15
Cook, James, 11, 38, 55, 59, 62; Great Southern Continent, search for, 40, 56–57; killing of in Hawaiian Islands, 57
Cooper, Whina, 106
cosmologies, 22, 39, 136; Hawaiian, 86; Inca, 42
critical analytic framework, 14
Crosby, Alfred, 78
cultural politics, 121
cultural pride and advocacy, 27
Cushman, Gregory, 79

Dampier, William, 55
D'Arcy, Paul, 127
debates and discussions, 14–15, 104
decolonization, 97–100
defamiliarization, 55
Defoe, Daniel, 56
Deng Xiaoping, 37
Diamond, Jared, 32, 87
diasporic communities, 138; China and, 127–28; Chinese, 38
Diaz, Vicente, 140
diffusionist models, 125
digital sources, 137–38
disease, 78–79, 136

DNA science, 20, 26, 131, 132
Doctor, Manilal Maganlal (activist), 92
domestic sphere, 82
Drake, Francis, 55
Dreaming realm, 71
drift net fishing, 103–4
Duff, Alan, 107, 139–40
Durr, Eveline, 85
d'Urville, Dumont, 28
Dutch East India Company (VOC), 41, 54
Dutch empire, 41, 53–54, 93, 123

East Asia, 9, 14, 85; Pacific leadership idea and, 123
Easter Island. *See* Rapa Nui/Easter Island
ecological imperialism, 78–79
ecological science, 32
economies, 52, 135; local, 74, 80, 98; Pacific Century, 123–25; testing and exams on, 134
Edo Bay (Japan), 74, 92
Education about Asia archive, 141
eighteenth century, 40, 44, 53–54
El Dorado, 57
empire: contingency of, 43–44; as imaginary, 70; as term, 68; as Western encroachment, 69–70
encounter and connection, points of, 11
Enlightenment, 40, 44; missionary enterprises, 59, 63–64; non-European-focused register, 60; as Pacific category, 54–62; Pacific influence on, 61–62; scientific progress, ideologies of, 59–60
Enrique (native guide), 46, 55
enslaved people, 52–53, 62; as guides, 46, 55
entrepreneurship/start-ups, 74
environmental issues, 5, 32, 41, 59, 101, 133; antinuclear movements, 102–3;

climate change, 40, 57, 121–23; engaging with, 121–23; marine products and creatures, 77–78
ethnology. *See* anthropology and ethnology as teaching tools
European empire, 4; as nineteenth-century phenomenon, 40–41
European explorers, 26, 38–42
European history, 9–10
Europeans, 38–42
everyday life, 22, 124; of labor, 81–85; during war, 96
exchange, 29, 31
Executive Order 9066 (Roosevelt), 15
exiles, 88
experience, 113–15
explorers: Chinese Treasure Fleets, 36–38; "discovery," concept of, 39, 40, 43; European, 30, 36; European reliance on Arab navigators, 39; French, 26, 28

Family Ingredients (Public Television series), 140–41
family lore, 1
fashion, 52–53
favoritism, 44
Fernández de Quirós, Pedro, 43
feudal society, 47
Fijian islands, 70, 72, 73–74, 83; anticolonial activism in, 92–93; Council of Great Chiefs, 106–7; Indian community in, 84; World War II and, 95–96
Filipino immigrants, 88
films/movies/documentaries, 62, 73, 75, 102, 107, 135, 139–41, 142
fishing, commercial, 103–4
folkloric images, 91
Follow the Rabbit-Proof Fence (Pilkington), 108

food customs, 124–25, 140–41
food safety and security, 124–25
foundational principles and stories, 7
French, 31, 53, 54, 70
friendship, 61
From a Native Daughter (Trask), 75
Frum, John (iconic figure/American GI), 114–15, 132

galleon trade, 51–53, 125
Gama, Vasco da, 39
Gandhi, Mohandas, 99
gender roles, 69, 82, 105–7
generational views, 13, 97; twenty-first century, 98
genetically modified organisms (GMOs), 125
geography, 35–36, 130; imperialism and, 85–88; Occidental perspective, 9, 13, 34
Germany, 95
Global Commodities, 138
global imperialism, 1; challenges to, 93–94
global issues, 102–3
globalization, 33–34; educational institutions and, 87; eighteenth century, 76–81; historical antecedents, 51–52, 60–61; mutiny on the *Bounty*, 62
globalization paradigm, 13
global perspectives, 2
"going native," 55–56
Golden Rice, 125
Google reference approach, 21
Great Southern Continent, 40, 56–57
Greenpeace, 103
guano, 79
gunboat diplomacy, 70

Half Life (movie), 102, 140
Hawai'i, 23; blood quantum debates, 131; Clinton's apology for U.S. seizure of, 109; Great Mahele land division, 68; Kamehameha lines, 30; Mexican community in, 85–86; Polynesian Cultural Center, 117
Hawaiian Islands, 57, 72; imperialism and, 72, 74–75; labor regimes in, 83; loss of indigenous sovereignty, 72
health policy, 136
hegemony, 68
Heisenberg uncertainty principle, 116
heroes, designation of, 46
heteroglossic spatiality, 132
Heyerdahl, Thor, 27
hierarchical societies, 29
Hiroo Onoda (straggler soldier), 109
historical thinking, 25–26
historiography, 44–45
history teachers, expansion of subject matter, 2
Ho Chi Minh, 99
Hōkūle'a (canoe) story, 26–27
homeland, 54
Hone Heke (warrior), 72–73
Hong Kong, 127
Houqua (Chinese trading master), 70
Humabon, Rajah, 46
Humboldt, Alexander von, 45

identities: fashion and, 53; nationalist, 91–94
identity as a teaching tool, 105–10; how groups and individuals define themselves, 105–8; justice in history, 108–10; sovereignty movements, 109–10
idyllic imaginary, 4
images, 113–17, 132, 141–42
imagined community, 93

immigration, 82–86, 88, 93, 117, 119, 143; Mexicans in Hawai'i, 85–86. *See also* migration

imperialism: as always evolving, 70–71; Asian, 74–75; chemical stimulants to enable physical labor, 80; commercial interests intertwined with, 75; as culture, 73; culture and identity, 73; ecological, 78–79; geography and, 85–88; globalization of commodities, 76–81; historical actors, 68–76; labor, everyday life of, 81–85; land appropriation, 71–72; newer imperial powers, 67–68; as teaching tool, 67–88; terms and definitions, 67; United States and, 68, 70, 72, 86; wars and, 92, 95; Western/European, 68. *See also* colonialism

Indian influences, 34, 36

Indian National Congress, 92

Indian Ocean, 9, 33–34, 35–36

indigenous societies, 53–54; Aboriginal peoples, 70, 71, 72

Indochina, 70

Indonesia, 29, 98; anticolonial struggles, 92; Java, 35; Muslim population, 36

influenza epidemic of 1918, 78

informants, local and regional, 46

institutions, 44

internet, 91, 138–39

intersection of historical periods, 5–6

introductory frameworks, 3

investigative approaches, languages, 22–23

Islam, 36–37

Islamic cultures, 36

island polities, 11

islands, as thought experiments, 32

isolation, 30

Italy, 95

Iwo Jima, Battle of, 4, 97, 133

Japan, 12; anime and manga, 47, 124; atomic bombs dropped on, 97, 101–2; economic leadership, 123–24; Edo, port of, 74, 92; imperial invasions by, 74; samurai era, 46–48; sixteenth century, 46–47; Tohoku earthquake (2011), 122–23; 2011 tsunami, 12; in World War II, 96–97; Yasukuni war memorial, 15

Java, 35

Jeoly (native informant), 55

Jesuit priests, Portuguese, 47–48

Jolly, Margaret, 106

Jones, Ryan, 78

justice, 108–10, 128

Kabutaulaka, Tara, 139

Kamehameha, King (Hawai'i), 69, 73

Kanaka Maoli (Hawaiian people), 57, 75, 85–86, 109, 130

Kartini (national heroine), 92

Kauanui, J. Kehaulani, 130

Kawainui Kane, Herb, 21–22

Kazu Maru (fishing vessel), 12

Kendrick, John, 69

Kennedy, John F., 97

key issues, 2

King Solomon's Mines, 57

kinship and exchanges, 61

knowledge, engaging with: digital sources, 137–38; environmental histories, 121–23; goals, 142–44; Pacific Century, 123–25; spokespersons, 128–31; testing and exams, 131–37

Kon-Tiki (raft), 27

Kora, 12

Korea, 74

Kula rings, 31, 90

Kwaisulia (Islander), 84

labor: actions, patterns of, 82–83; everyday life of, 81–85, 104; forced migration and, 118–19; transnational, 118
labor organizations, 83
Lander, Joan, 140
languages, 22–23, 132
Lapita cultures, 28
Lapita pottery style, 20
Lapu Lapu (chieftain), 46
Latin America, 9
launching questions, 2
lecture format, 132
Lee Kuan Yew, 123
legendary figures, 37
legends, 56–57
Lindstrom, Lamont, 114
linguistic investigations, 22–23
Lin Zexu, 79
literature, 58, 107–8
lived experience. *See* everyday life
living principle, 8
living worlds, historical worlds as, 35
local politics, 100–101
London Missionary Society, 63
lunas (overseers), 83

Macao, 40, 41
MacArthur, Douglas, 97
Made in Taiwan (movie), 131
Magellan, Ferdinand de, 38, 39, 45–46
Makasserese peoples, 72
Malaspina, Alejandro, 45
Malaysia, 36
Malinowski, Bronislaw, 90
Manchuria, 15
"mandala" political rule, 14
Manila, 52, 125
Maori people, 73
Mao Zedong, 97–98, 99
maps, 12–14, 33–34; eighteenth century, 55; imaginary components, 39–40; religious worldviews and, 39–40
Maquinna (chief of Nootka Sound), 61
Marcos, Ferdinand, 88, 105
Maretu (Islander preacher), 64
Mariner, William, 55
maritime imagination, 25
Maritime Silk Road initiative, 125
material contexts, 6; islands as experiments, 32; labor, everyday life of, 81–82
material culture objects, 91
Matisoo-Smith, Lisa, 20
Mau Piailug, 27
Mead, Margaret, 32, 90, 132
Mediterranean studies, 33
Melaka (Malacca), 35–36, 40, 41; siege of, 46
Melanesia, 114; terminology of, 28
Melville, Herman, 58
memoirs, 142–43
Mendaña, Álvaro de, 43, 44
methodology, 59–60
Mexican-American War, 68
Mexican community in Hawai'i, 85–86
Mexico, 42, 43, 52
microhistorical case approach, 14
Micronesia, terminology of, 28
migration, 117–18; ancient, 4–5, 10–11, 22, 25–26, 28, 30, 60; Chinese, 85; Lapita cultures, 28. *See also* immigration
military forces, 41
military history, 96–97
millenarian movements, 99
Miner, Horace, 55
mining, 104
Mirnha (Caterina de San Juan), 52–53
missionary enterprises, 59; native agents, 63–64, 133
mixed identities, 37

INDEX

Moana (Disney Studios), 140
mobility, 23, 28; as forced displacement, 118–19
Moby Dick (Melville), 58
Molisa, Grace, 106–7, 132
monsoon winds, 36
Monterey, port at, 43
Moro National Liberation Front (Philippines), 119
multinational corporations, 41
multiple perspectives, 4–5
Murnau, F. W., 140
Murphy, Geoff, 73, 139
museum collections, 21, 60, 90–91, 129, 136; Aboriginal remains, 130; online, 138
music, 107
Muslim populations, 36
mutiny on the *Bounty*, 62, 67
mystery narrative, 87
mythic realities, 19–20

Napoleonic wars, 70
narrations, 83–85
nationalist identities, 91–94, 136
National Library of Australia, 138
Native Americans, 52; blood quantum debates, 131; Nootka Sound, 61; Pacific Northwest, 75–76
Native Mother, 132
natural history, 61, 135
nature, state of, 54–55
navigation, 25–29, 136; drift currents, 26; intentional, questioning of, 26–27
Nazism, 95
Nehru-Gandhi family, 30
networks, 9, 11, 29, 30–31; of communicators, 99; political actors, 87; postwar conflict and, 99
New Caledonia, 104

New Guinea, 31
New Silk Road, 125–26
New Spain (Mexico), 42, 43, 52
New Zealand, 70, 72–73; administrative knowledge and practice, 125; Christchurch shootings, 120; sealing, 75; Union Steam Ship Company, 80
noble savages, 53, 54
North America, 9
Northwest Passage, 40, 57

Obeyesekere, Gananath, 57
Occidental perspective, 9, 13, 34
Oceanian island peoples, 9
Oceanian perspectives, 11
Okeanos Foundation for the Sea, 142
Omai (island voyager), 56
Once Were Warriors (Duff), 107, 139–40
online collections, 138
opium/opiates, 79–80
Opium Wars, 70, 79, 133
oral histories, 96, 97
oral traditions, 8, 19–20
orang laut (person of the sea), 35
orangutans, 35, 37
organizations, 44
origin tales, 26
O'Rourke, Dennis, 140
otter pelts, 77
outsider's perspective, 3
overfishing, 103–4, 124
overviews, 12

Pacific: bigger picture, 4–5; definitions, 9, 10–11; isolation, ideas of, 28, 30, 51, 56, 60–61; network approach, 9; trans-pacific, 85
Pacific Century, 5, 123–25, 135, 143
Pacific-facing regions, 85
Pacific history, lack of conventions, 10

INDEX

Pacific Islanders in Communications, 140
Pacific Islands, 8–9; influenza epidemic of 1918, 78; vanishing territory, 121–22
Pacific Island studies, 11, 12; evolution of, 8
Pacific Northwest, 75–76, 88
Pacific Ocean, naming of, 38, 45
Pacific orientation, 34
Pacific Rim, 9, 85, 135; Pacific leadership idea, 123–25
Pacific Rim approach, 33
Pacific War (World War II), 95–97, 109, 125, 134–35; legacies of, 113
Pacific Way, 121–23, 143
Panama Canal, 70
Papua New Guinea, 140
Parameswara (Shah Iskandar), 35–36
patriotism, 93
Pearl Harbor, bombing of, 4, 96
People Power (Philippines), 105
performance, 8, 27–28, 132
Perry, Matthew, 70, 92
Peru, 42, 52
pharmaceuticals, spices compared with, 41–42
phenotypes, 28
Philippines, 36, 43, 88, 98; contemporary politics, 119; identity in, 105; Tasaday people, 115–16
Pilkington, Doris, 108
pirates, 48–49, 55
Pitcairn island, 62
plantation crops and systems, 75, 78, 83–84; chemical stimulants, 80
Pohnpei civilization, 31
political actors, 87
political systems, 29
politics, contemporary, 119–20
Polynesia, 20, 31; plantation crops and imperialism in, 75; terminology of, 12–13, 28
Polynesian Cultural Center (Oahu, Hawai'i), 117
Polynesian Panthers, 99
Polynesian Voyaging Society, 26–27
popular culture, 2, 90–91, 107–8, 135
ports, 35–36
Portuguese navigators, 39, 43, 45; Jesuit priests, 47–48
preservation discourses, 129
primary sources, 59, 137–38
"primitive," the, 89–90, 114–16
private property, 71–72
public health policy, 78–79, 136
Puhipau, Abraham, 140

race, discussions of, 28–29, 136; anti-immigrant, 82; atomic bombing of Japan, 97; black-white-Latino triangle, 86
radiation exposure, 101–2
Radio Bikini (movie), 102
Ra'iatean Omai, 54
Rainbow Warrior (protest ship), 103
Rapa Nui/Easter Island, 20, 32, 87, 136
Rape of Nanjing legacies, 15, 96, 109
realities, mythic, 19–20
Real Principe Chinese mestizo regiment, 44
reconstructions, 6, 10, 20–23, 26, 28, 44, 76; labor, 82–83; material culture objects used for, 91
refugees, 118
Reid, Joshua, 76
religion, 63–64, 136; faith converts, 52–53; "godly mechanics," 63; millenarian movements, 99; missionary enterprises, 59, 63–64; "native agents," 63–64

Renaissance maps, 39–40
Renaissance views of Pacific, 58–59
representations and realities, 113–20, 136; experience vs. image, 113–15; images, 113–17; of primitive, 115–18
resistance, 46, 73, 92, 93, 95; antisettler and anticolonial struggles, 91–94
resource extraction, 104
revisionism, 45
revitalization projects, 129
revolutions, 93–94
Rivoli, Petra, 77
Robinson Crusoe (Defoe), 56
role-plays, 29–30
Roosevelt, Franklin, 15
Russo-Japanese wars (1904–5), 92
Ryukyu Islands, 129

Sacred Vessels (documentary), 140
Sahlins, Marshall, 57
sailors, 82
Samoa, 31, 32, 90; World War II and, 95–96
Samoan archipelago, 23
samurai, 46–48
Sanadhya, Totaram (Fijian activist), 92
San Vitores, Diego Luis de, 44–45
Sarawak (Borneo), 72
Sarekat Islam (group, Indonesia), 93
scarcity, 32
scholars and scholarship, 3, 11–12, 126–27; on atomic testing, 102; newer studies, 86–87
scholarship, performance as, 8
Schorch, Philipp, 85
science, 26, 32, 44, 55, 135; botanical interest, 41–42, 61, 62
scientific progress, ideologies of, 59–60
sea cucumber/trepang, 76–77, 83
Sea Is My Country, The (Reid), 76

Seattle, 88
Senkaku/Diaoyu Islands, 15
settler colonialism, 68
Seven Years' War, 44, 45, 53
shipping, 81–82
Siddhartha Guatama (Buddha), 34–35
sidebars, 13
Silk Road, 42
Silk Road Economic Belt, 125
silver coinage, 52
simplicity, Western concepts of, 54, 90; during war, 96
Sinbad the Sailor, 37
Singapore, 123
Sino-Japanese war (1894–95), 92, 95
slavery, 32, 49, 62, 108–9
social media, 91, 138
societies, 29–32
Solis, Gabriel, 106
Solomon Islands, 96–97
Sorry Day (Australia), 15, 108
South America, 9, 22, 85
South Asia, 12
South China Sea, 35–36, 48; Chinese military installments, 127
Southeast Asia, 9, 12
South Pacific, 60
sovereignty movements, 109–10
Soviet-American tensions, 98
Spain, Seven Years' War, 44, 45, 53
Spanish-American War, 45
Spanish empire, 123; galleon trade, 51–53
Spanish intellectuals, 45
Spanish Lake, 43–44, 53; Black Legend interpretation, 45; non-Spanish actors in, 44
Spanish navigators, 39, 40, 42–46, 45
Spice Islands, 41
spices, 41–42, 45

INDEX

Sri Lanka, 37, 120
standard narrative, 9–10
state of nature, 54–55
Steel, Frances, 81
stereotypes, 28–29; paradise, 31–32; simple lives, 32
Stolen Generation (Australia), 108
Stone, Robert, 102, 140
Strait of Melaka (Malacca), 34, 35–36
stranger worship, debate on, 57
student friendliness as approach, 13
students, beginning in contemporary period of, 19–20
Sun Yat-sen, 93
supply chains, 41–42, 51–52, 77, 132–33; British, 90
surveys, 14
sustainability, 32
syllabus, 7
synchronic and diachronic discussions, 10

tabu (kapu/tapu/tabu/taboo), 57, 132
Tahiti, 54, 62; Pomare, 30
Taiwan, 74, 99; Austronesian renaissance, 126, 128, 131
Tanna (Melanesian island), 114
tapa cloth, 60
Tasaday people (Philippines), 115–16
Tauʻufa (Islander preacher), 64
teaching what you think you know, 1–7
terminologies, 12–13, 28
Terra Australis Incognita (map), 40
terrorism, 119
testing and exams, 131–37; entry points, 135–36; final project, 136–37; interdisciplinary context, 134; project-based learning, 135; vocabularies, 134–36
Te Wheke (Maori warrior), 73, 139
textbooks, 9–10, 70
textile production, 77

themes, 12
thinking beyond discipline, 7–15
Thompson, Nainoa, 27
thought experiments, 32
time and space, exploration of, 2, 14, 19
Tohoku earthquake (Japan, 2011), 122–23
Tonga, 31
Tongan archipelago, 23
Tongan islands, 55
Tordesillas, Treaty of, 43
touchstones, 5–6
tourism, 113, 116–18, 135, 140
town-hall model, 104
trade: imperialism and, 75–76; plantation crops, 75, 78, 80, 83–84
transformation over time, 42
Trask, Haunani-Kay, 75
Trask sisters (Hawaiʻi), 106
travel approach, 13–14, 32, 35
Travels of a T-Shirt in the Global Economy, The (Rivoli), 77
Trobriand Islanders, 31
Trobriand Islands, 90
Twitter, 138
Typee (Melville), 58

Union Steam Ship Company (New Zealand), 80
United States, 12, 15; Hawaiʻi, relationship to, 85–86; imperialism, 68, 70, 72, 86; Pacific Northwest, 75–76; political activism in, 88
universities, legacy of slavery and, 108–9
University of Hawaiʻi, 75, 126, 138; visual sources, 139
utopian projects, 32
Utu (movie), 73, 139

vanished cultures discourse, 129–30
Vanuatu, 106

Versailles decisions, 99
Vietnam, 70, 99; refugees, 118
visual exercises, 133
Vouza, Jacob, 96

Waitangi, Treaty of, 72
war: American Civil War, 83–84; atomic warfare, 97, 101–3; Islanders as active participants in, 95–96; lived experience of, 96; Mexican-American War, 68; Napoleonic wars, 70; Opium Wars, 70, 79; Pacific War (World War II), 95–97, 109, 113; Russo-Japanese wars (1904–5), 92; Seven Years' War, 44, 45, 53; shaping of history and, 95–97; Sino-Japanese war (1894–95), 92, 95; Spanish-American War, 45; Yasukuni war memorial (Japan), 15
Western approaches to teaching history, 8, 9, 39
Western civilization studies, 31
whaling, 78, 83
Wiener, Michael, 12
Williams, John, 63

women: in anticolonial struggles, 92; antinuclear movements and, 102; environmental movements and, 104; in politics, 105–6; sexual abuse of, 15, 96, 109, 128–29; war crimes and, 108
World and All the Things upon It, The (Chang), 86
world history, 36
World History Association, 138
world systems, 51–64; ritual understandings, 57–58; Spanish galleon trade, 51–53
World Trade Center attack (2001), 119–20
World War II, 95–97, 109, 113, 125, 134–35
wrongs, historical, 15

Xi Jinping, 125

Yap, island of, 31
Yasukuni war memorial (Japan), 15

Zheng He, 36–37, 125, 133

www.ingramcontent.com/pod-product-compliance
Lightning Source LLC
Chambersburg PA
CBHW021858230426
43671CB00006B/441